Selling Out America's Children

How America Puts Profits Before
Values—and What Parents Can Do

David Walsh, Ph.D.

Best wishes
Dave Walsh

FAIRVIEW PRESS
(FORMERLY KNOWN AS DEACONESS PRESS)
Minneapolis

Published by Fairview Press (a service of Fairview Riverside Medical Center, a division of Fairview Hospital and Healthcare Services), 2450 Riverside Avenue South, Minneapolis, MN 55454.

Library of Congress Cataloging-in-Publication Data

Walsh, David Allen.
    Selling out America's Children : how America puts profits before values—and what parents can do / David Walsh.
        p.   cm.
    Includes index.
    ISBN 0-925190-27-6 : $11.95
    1. Mass media and children—United States—Moral and ethical aspects.   2. Children—United States—Attitudes.   3. Children as consumers—United States.   4. United States--Moral conditions.
    5. Parenting—United States.   I. Title.
HQ784.M3W35   1994
305.23'083—dc20
94-14004

CIP

First paperback printing: January, 1995

Printed in the United States of America

99 98 97 96 95   7 6 5 4 3 2 1

Cover design by *Circus Design*
Interior design by *The Nancekivell Group*

Publisher's Note: Fairview Press (formerly known as Deaconess Press) publishes books and other materials related to the subjects of physical health, mental health, and chemical dependency. Its publications, including *Selling Out America's Children*, do not necessarily reflect the philosophy of Fairview Hospital and Healthcare Services or its treatment programs.

Children are the purpose of life.
We were once children
and someone cared for us.
Now it is our time to care.

— a Cree Elder

CONTENTS

I have heard that phrase—"there's nothing you can do"—many times over the past seven years. I have heard it spoken by parents who are concerned about their children's welfare yet feel their actions don't make a dent in the forces working against them. In spite of their frustration, however, they desperately want to do *something!*

As I have talked with these parents, I have been struck by how much consensus there is among them as to the important values children must learn. I have also been struck by the fact that the set of values they identify is not the one that is supported in our larger society.

This dichotomy between private and societal values has become clearer in meeting after meeting, and I have begun using it as the basis for a new seminar. Once again, at the urging of parents and educators, I have decided to convert the substance of the seminar, along with the discussions I've had with parents and other concerned adults, into a book.

While I believe our children are in trouble because of what we, as a society, have taught them (and have failed to teach them), I also believe that there is reason for hope. My optimism is based on my interactions with so many adults who have not forgotten what values are essential for healthy children. Those values have not been forgotten, but they have become lost in a larger, anonymous society where a different set of values has been promoted— a set that is designed to raise profits, not children.

INTRODUCTION

In 1987, I developed a seminar for parents entitled "Designer Kids." Based on my experiences both as a psychologist and as a parent of three children, I had a growing concern about the effects of excess competition and consumerism on America's children. The seminar dealt with those effects. At the urging of many of those who attended the seminars, I converted the content of the presentation into a book by the same title, which was published by Deaconess Press in 1990.

In the four years since the appearance of that book, I have had the opportunity to make many more presentations across the country to groups of parents, educators, and other professionals who work with youth. Several things have become very clear in gathering after gathering. No matter where I have gone, and without exception, I have heard a great deal of concern about the seeming lack of positive values in America's children. Whether I was talking with parents who spoke to me at PTA meetings or participants on radio call-in shows, the theme was (and continues to be) the same: a widespread concern that America's children are in trouble.

While parents and educators have expressed their anxieties, they have also expressed feelings of helplessness and confusion. Many feel isolated and alone as they try to turn back a river of cultural forces that they sense are hostile to the healthy development of children. At the same time, they fear that there is nothing they can do that will make a difference.

ACKNOWLEDGMENTS

The ideas expressed in this book took shape as the result of many conversations with groups of parents, friends, and colleagues over a period of years. There are too many to recognize individually, and there are some whose names I do not even know. Still, I would like to thank those people.

I also would like to thank the staff at Deaconess Press for their expertise, support, and hard work, especially Jack Caravela for his excellent assistance with the manuscript.

I would like to thank my three children: Dan, Brian, and Erin for their patience, as I devoted many hours to this endeavor.

Most of all, I would like to acknowledge the enormous contributions of my wife, Monica. She played an integral role in all phases of this project. She helped with research, she challenged my ideas, and she spent hours on the manuscript. Most important to me, she was a source of support and encouragement. This book is dedicated to her.

The good news is that since America's adults largely agree on the healthy values our children should learn, we can not only take responsibility for teaching them to our children, but can do so in practical and effective ways. We can exert our right to influence the voices of our larger society so that profit is unseated as the great motivator and the welfare of our children becomes the primary concern once again.

The growing awareness of violence in our society, especially among children, seems to be finally waking us up. However, it would be a mistake to think that violence is the only problem. It isn't. It is a tragic symptom of an underlying crisis that involves an entire set of values being taught to our children. We will only begin to make progress when we see the whole problem for what it is. Violence grabs the headlines, but violence itself is a result of a society that promotes selfishness, greed, and instant gratification.

While we must do whatever we can to curb the epidemic of violence, we must also recognize that we won't be successful until we begin to reprioritize our values as a society and once again take our responsibility to our children seriously.

It is my hope that this book will make a contribution to that undertaking. Parents and other concerned adults can make a difference; this book will show how. The first step is to become fully aware of what we are facing.

CHAPTER 1

The Alarms Are Sounding. Is Anybody Listening?

Does this story sound familiar?
A colleague of mine was traveling with his family on a long-awaited summer vacation trip to California. When they finished the four-day automobile trip from Minnesota, a message was waiting for them to call home right away—it was an emergency. The phone call brought dreaded news. There had been big trouble, and they were told that they had better come home right away.

My colleague's vacation was over before it began. His family's home had been broken into, robbed, and vandalized almost as soon as they had departed. Their house had become "party central" for several days for dozens of teenagers who ate the family's food, broke their furniture, stole their valuables, wore their clothes, defaced their home's walls, and defecated and urinated on their carpets.

The family was devastated, and felt both cheated and violated. Each member tried to think of clues as to who might have done this to them, and for what reason.

Within several days the police had pieced together the story. The thousands of dollars worth of damage to the home had been done by youngsters only vaguely known to the family. Dozens of young people had been involved, but only the four ringleaders were arrested. Their motives did not include a grudge against the family; when asked why they did it, they said, "It was just for fun."

The idea that a group of kids would commit these crimes with no real motive was shocking enough to my colleague, but he received another surprise: the organizers of the theft and destruction of nearly all his family's possessions were seniors at one of the most prestigious private schools in the Twin Cities.

Several days after hearing this account from my colleague, I had occasion to overhear a conversation between two elementary school-age boys on the sidewalk in front of my house. I was doing some yard work nearby as I heard one of them—a polite but shy nine-year-old—enthusiastically describe to his friend a new video game he owned. (I later learned that the game was called Mortal Kombat, and was one of the top-selling video games on the market.) This young boy was describing how, after hours of practice, he was now able to cut the enemy's head off, rip out his heart, and snap his spine, delivering the most lethal blows the game had to offer. Both boys were very excited, and were hurrying home to the first boy's house to "play."

Stories like these should be alarms to us. We often don't recognize them as such, probably because they are so commonplace in the America of the 1990s. Sometimes we don't hear the alarms even when we are confronted with the litany of disturbing statistics concerning America's children.

For instance, the Children's Defense Society has documented that:

- Gun violence takes a child's life in the United States every three hours.
- Every nine minutes, a child is arrested for a drug/alcohol offense.
- Every minute of every day, an American teenager has a baby. (This is the highest rate in the industrialized world.)
- Every twenty-six seconds an American child runs away from home.

Other sources have recorded the following:

- Suicide is the third leading cause of death among young people.
- A 1990 Gallup survey found that fifteen percent of teenagers had considered suicide at some time, and that six percent had actually attempted it.
- The American Medical Association issued a white paper report in 1990 indicating that sixteen percent of male youth and nineteen percent of female youth in the United States suffer from depression.

These statistics have human faces. Take John, for instance. John was interviewed by a television reporter doing an in-depth newscast on homeless teenagers. John had been on the street for five months, panhandling. "I just live for today," he explained. John had left home because he could no longer tolerate the verbal and physical abuse directed at him by his father. John was fifteen years old at the time of the interview.

The statistics go on:

- Twenty percent of all American children are living below the poverty line.
- Two and one half million children in the United States do not have permanent homes.

Alice is four years old. She and her one-year-old brother have moved more than ten times in the past year. In good weather, they and their mother would spend many nights in their parked car. Once winter came, they would go to a shelter for the homeless. Alice likes the shelter because she can meet other kids, and because she likes the peanut butter sandwiches she gets there.

- The national high school dropout rate is approaching twenty-five percent.
- As a national average, SAT scores have dropped seventy points in the past three decades.

Ron is a very capable high school student, but doesn't want to sign up for algebra classes at his high school. Instead, he enrolls in the basic math course because he thinks it will be easier. "Algebra is too hard. Besides, I'm not going to be a mathematician." Ron could handle algebra with no great difficulty if he was willing to put in some time studying and doing homework. Ron's parents don't pay attention to his class selection.

- Twenty-five percent of American girls and thirty-three percent of American boys have had sexual intercourse by the time they are fifteen years old.
- Ten thousand babies a year are born to girls in the U.S. under the age of fifteen.

Joe is fifteen years old and a father. He sees his girlfriend and his son "once in a while." He explains that he and his girlfriend are not getting along very well anymore. They have lots of arguments and it's not nearly as much fun as it used to be before their baby was born. When I ask him about his son, he seems uninterested. He assures me that the baby will be okay because his girlfriend's parents are taking care of him. When I ask if he thinks he will spend a lot of time with his son as he grows up, he tells me he doesn't think so. "Her parents are going to raise him."

- Junior and senior high school students drink thirty-five percent of all the wine coolers sold in the United States.
- 41.2% of youth report use of tobacco in some form.
- A 1991 Surgeon General's report noted that sixteen percent of America's junior and senior high school youth drink alcohol weekly, and that almost a half million of them have five or more consecutive drinks at least once a week.

Jane's friends gather to drink on Friday nights. Jane is fourteen. The favorite hangout is at the lake outside town. The police have been called several times, but everyone scatters as soon as the squad car is seen. Some of the parents know what's going on but either don't appear concerned or aren't able to stop it. Jane herself has been grounded numerous times in the past, but just ignores the groundings. As soon as her parents are distracted, she's out the door again. When she comes home, there are shouting matches and threats, but nothing changes. Her parents have brought her to the school counselor. Jane thinks her parents should just "chill out" and "get off her back." Jane acknowledges that sexual activity is common at the drinking parties.

- More than five percent of American school children carry a gun.
- 3.6 million high school students are physically assaulted annually, most by other adolescents.
- More teenage boys die of gunshot wounds than all other causes of death combined.
- Violent crime among fifteen-year-old American males has increased by 264 percent over the past four years.

Tim's high school has police in the hallways and surveillance in the parking lot. It wasn't always like that. When his older brother went to the same school seven years earlier, none of those security measures were in place. But a steady increase in assaults and weapons violations prompted school board reactions. The year before these security measures were taken, a gang-related confrontation in the school cafeteria resulted in multiple injuries.

The alarms aren't only to be heard in the lives of children and in statistics concerning youth. If we look, we also see them in the choices and events of our own daily lives:

• We install security devices in our homes and cordon off our yards with fences to protect ourselves from our neighbors.
• Our schools are building concrete walls around playgrounds to protect children from such dangers as stray bullets fired by gangs.
• Suburban school districts are equipping elementary school buses with surveillance cameras to reduce assaults and property damage.
• We hear news stories like those about the murder of James Jordan, father of NBA star Michael Jordan. Two teenagers were charged.
• Our kids are afraid to wear certain clothes to school for fear they will be robbed.

The economic and psychological costs of crime and social problems in our daily lives are staggering. America's annual expenditure in public funds for teenage pregnancy alone exceeds twenty billion dollars a year, and we can't build detention centers for kids quickly enough. As we try to fund programs to help the most acutely distressed young people, the stress on our health care and social welfare budgets has reached the breaking point.

As serious as the situation is, however, a glimpse into the future is even more frightening. The problems are all increasing, and resources are scarce already. How did this happen? How did we get ourselves into this mess? The ugly truth is that we, as a society, did it to ourselves. Although these consequences were never what we intended, America's adults have caused this state of circumstances for our kids. This book is an attempt to explain how we are selling out our kids without realizing we're doing it, and how we can stop it.

Today's generation of young people is a relatively small one demographically. The front edge of the population bulge known as the "baby boom" is now approaching age fifty. As the 21st century progresses, a bulge of retired citizens will depend on today's children for support. So from a purely selfish point of view, we cannot afford to write off millions of today's youth as illiterate, violent, undereducated, emotionally disturbed, or socially deviant. If we do, we will be abandoning the very persons whom we will be asking to support us in our retirement. And if your response is that you are planning not to be financially dependent upon your own children or on social security, remember that our government, national economy, and social institutions are only as strong as the current taxpaying workforce.

The motivation for action is not only economic. The very survival of our society and of fundamental American values depends on responsible, productive, and generous citizens. Those types of citizens don't just happen—they are guided, nurtured, and raised. If we are to preserve the foundations of our society, we have no choice but to act now. It is not alarmist rhetoric to say that the future is at stake. It is reality.

A natural temptation is to look for a scapegoat when things are not going well. Since things are not going well with our kids, the search for a scapegoat is in high gear. Parents blame teachers. Teachers blame parents. Both blame political leaders, who in turn blame one another. Most tragically of all, in our frustration we often blame the kids.

Larry Brendtro, Martin Brokenleg, and Steve Van Bockern, the authors of a book titled *Reclaiming Youth at Risk,* make an accurate assessment:

"Alienated children and youth are assigned a multitude of labels, most of them unfriendly. They are described as aggressive or anxious, as attention-disordered or affectionless, as unmotivated or unteachable, as drug abusers or dropouts. Most terms are either overtly hostile or covertly patronizing in the long-established tradition of blaming the victim."

This statement is not directed at the layperson, but at professionals who deal with youth. As a professional counselor of adolescents and their families, I can vouch for the fact that much of the current literature on today's youth is negative, pessimistic and cynical. And if this reflects the perspective of those whose careers are devoted to today's youth, we can imagine that of society in general.

One thing is for sure: there is enough blame to go around for everyone. But placing blame on any group is not going to get us anywhere. What can lead to change is our taking responsibility for what has happened and for what will happen from this point onward.

I have stated several times already that the responsibility for what has happened to our kids rests with us. Let me make it clear that I am not blaming all, or even most parents for not trying to instill values in their own children. As I talk with parents across the country, I find, by and large, good people trying their best to raise their children as well as they can. I believe that my wife and I are doing the same. Yet I still contend that we are all responsible for selling out America's kids.

There is a very important distinction to be made here—the distinction between individual responsibility and societal responsibility. I believe that understanding that distinction is key. If we as a society are exploiting our children for profit, as I believe we are, then we need to examine what we can do as individuals to change the society we live in. There is no more important deliberation confronting us than how we, both as individuals and as a society, will raise our children.

CHAPTER 2

Moral Parents and Immoral Society

In 1932, a philosopher and theologian named Reinhold Niebuhr wrote a book entitled *Moral Man and Immoral Society*. Dr. Niebuhr drew a very important distinction between the moral behavior of an individual and the immoral behavior of a larger social group.

As individuals, we have certain rules of behavior in our personal relationships. We can observe and assess the impact of our actions on the other person, and based on the effects of our behavior, we can modify future decisions. We can consider the needs of the other person and judge the emotional and personal impact of our behavior. Through personal relationships we can develop empathy and may even forego our own needs at times for the sake of another person.

In larger groups, however, that dynamic is absent. In an individual's mind, the number of people involved may mitigate the effects of his or her actions. For instance, if I steal money from you, I may be able to directly observe and empathize with the impact of my actions on a personal level. If I steal money from a large financial institution, on the other hand, I need not be aware of the impact on any individual. Theft may take on a faceless, anonymous quality, even though individuals are still affected. The difference is that I do not personally observe the effects of my actions, which allows me to downplay their immoral nature.

Going a step further, when I steal money from an institution, even if I am unaware of the impact on any individual, I am aware of the fact that I did steal. I am able to judge the morality of my personal act against my standards of right and wrong even if I have rationalized my behavior. However, if the group I belong to steals money, my sense of personal responsibility may be diminished. Depending on how big the group is, my own sense of responsibility can melt into nothingness. Also, the rationalizations of a group for committing immoral acts can be much more convincing than our own personal ones. When we see that others accept them, we are more comfortable with them ourselves.

This dynamic explains how individuals often act in ways as part of a large group that they never would alone. The sense of responsibility gets weaker as the group gets larger, as do the odds that any one person will be singled out for blame later. Consequently, large groups sometimes act in ways that individuals within the group might find morally objectionable in another setting.

This phenomenon is the reason, for example, that thousands of people can participate in violent rampages such as the Los Angeles riots while in their normal everyday lives they are law-abiding citizens. It explains how large numbers of people can cheat phone companies with pirated long distance credit card numbers, and why many business people cheat on expense reports. These people might act very honestly in a one-on-one situation, but in a more anonymous setting, the sense of moral responsibility evaporates.

Actually, it is very difficult for a large group to act in a consistently moral way. The decision of a large group is often the distillation of many different judgments, needs, and opinions, and is made to serve the majority of its members in most cases. A group is less able to judge the impact of its decisions and actions on individuals, particularly those outside the group. When the group is as large as American society itself, it rarely if ever judges the validity of its needs by the needs of an individual person.

When the group decision harms an individual or a small minority, it becomes a case of the old saying, "You can't fight city hall." City hall may exist to serve the community, but it may not care about you as an individual.

Just as a large group is less able to balance its needs with those of individuals, it is also less able to control its need for self-gratification. The needs or the values of the large group will carry the day, and the largest or most powerful forces within the group will greatly influence those perceived needs and values.

This phenomenon is very powerful and can be very dangerous. Individuals who are part of a larger group must constantly examine whether the values or behavior of the larger group reasonably reflects their own values and whether the values and behavior of the group are good or correct within the context of their personal ideas of morality.

How does this apply to our discussion of what's happening to America's kids? I believe that the values of the larger, anonymous society we live in have become diametrically opposed to the values most American parents want to teach their children.

This is particularly dangerous because of the role society plays in child rearing. As crucial as the family is to preserving civilization, it has historically always been the larger group—the "tribe" rather than the nuclear family—that ultimately ensures cultural survival. Throughout history, some biological parents have always been absent or unreliable. Some die when their children are young; others are too immature or too irresponsible to effectively rear their offspring. In these situations, the "tribe" must assume responsibility and nourish the young.

However, there is a myth in our present culture that the responsibility for raising children belongs solely to individual parents in nuclear families. Sure, we have institutions like churches, schools, and social service agencies to help. But we have lost our attention to the influence that our society has on childrearing.

In past generations, the voice of the tribe would reinforce that of the parent, or fill in when a parent could not or would not pass on the mores of the group. Today, however, the voice of society contradicts the messages of individual parents. Rather than reinforce them, the larger society undermines and overwhelms the messages of parents, churches, schools, and other agencies designed to help keep our society intact. What is even more alarming is that the voices of our larger society often promote messages that are at odds with the bedrock values of our democratic civilization.

This discussion of values is at the heart of parenting. Barbara Dafoe Whitehead of the Institute for American Values conducted a series of interviews with parents in both individual and group settings. When asked what their most basic responsibilities as parents were, there was unanimity in the response, which can be summed up as "Putting a roof over my children's heads and teaching my kids right from wrong."

This down-to-earth description of the basic tasks of parenting is universal. It speaks to the dual responsibility of meeting both the physical and moral needs of our children. The importance of feeding, clothing, and protecting our sons and daughters is obvious. "Teaching my kids right from wrong" involves personal values that will help them get along in life, but it is just as essential for our society is to survive.

The problem comes in when the notions of right and wrong held by the majority of American parents are not reinforced by the voices of the larger society. In the following pages we will examine how and why society contradicts and overwhelms the moral messages of parents.

Overmatched Parents

The dichotomy between societal and parental messages has become more pronounced because the communication tools that our society has at its disposal have become so powerful. Parents, churches and schools try to pass on values by teaching, by example, and by talking to children. These methods pale in comparison with the powerful tools of persuasion of the modern electronic age. The thunderous, anonymous voices of our society include television, radio, print media, computers and video games, all employing increasingly sophisticated advertising strategies and technology.

If the values of our larger society matched those of individual parents, then these tools could be enlisted to reinforce moral values. Unfortunately, that is not the case.

The basic disparity comes down to this: what motivates individual parents is, as we have already mentioned, the desire to "teach my kids right from wrong." What motivates our larger, anonymous society is one thing: financial profit.

The overriding question in our society is, "Will it make money?" If an enterprise will increase profits, then all else becomes irrelevant, including the question of whether something is good or bad for children. Any initial qualms are quickly rationalized or explained away, if indeed they ever come up. The only operative question is "Will it be profitable?"

As a society, we Americans of the late twentieth century are sacrificing our children at the altar of financial gain. We are selling out America's children for money. Although we are often not consciously aware of it, maximizing profit is more important to us than asking ourselves whether or not something is beneficial or harmful to our children.

Our attitudes about violence are a clear case in point. On the one hand, there is a growing fear that violence may destroy our society. Individual Americans try to teach their children cooperation and nonviolent conflict resolution. At the same time, however, our society promotes violence. The tragic irony is that our larger anonymous society loves the very violence that we as individuals are afraid will destroy us. As a society, we encourage the use of violence for entertainment.

We will discuss the supporting evidence for this statement in a later chapter. For now, consider one fact: the average American child will witness two hundred thousand acts of violence on television before he or she is eighteen years old. As we shall see in Chapter Six, the documented correlation between violent entertainment and violent behavior is undeniable. By targeting violent entertainment at children, we are promoting their violent behavior—the very behavior we fear.

The issue of violent entertainment is a tragically clear example of the fundamental dichotomy between the values of individual Americans and those of our larger society. We are afraid, on the one hand, that violence will destroy our country. Day after day we say that it must stop, and we demand solutions from police and politicians. And yet we are simultaneously encouraging it, promoting it, and teaching it. Individually we hate it; as a society, we love it.

The reason for these insanely contradictory messages is very simple. What motivates us individually when we decry violence is our need for personal safety for ourselves and our children, and the survival of our communities. What motivates our larger society has nothing to do with the survival of faceless individuals or the good of our children. What motivates our anonymous society is one thing: money. Violent entertainment is aimed at children because it is profitable. Questions of right or wrong, beneficial or harmful, are not considered. The only question is, "Will it sell?"

As you are reading this, people are working on the latest video games for kids. Artists, writers, programmers, marketing professionals, and others work long hours to come up with something more appealing to kids, and most are not asking themselves whether their games are too violent or whether their creations will help or harm children. They are only asking themselves if they will sell and create profits. In their private lives, I would expect that many of these same people are parents who are concerned about what is good for their own children. But as part of a larger anonymous group creating violent video entertainment, such concerns are out of place. A creator of a violent video game might not let his or her own child play it, but even if this is the case, there is no sense of responsibility to the millions of other children who will. If the potential for profit is large enough, the game will be produced, regardless of its effect on children.

This is but one example of how we as a society are selling out America's children. Unfortunately, there are many others. What is behind all of them is the pursuit of money and profit.

An American child in the 1990s is bombarded with thousands of value messages every day. We see messages on billboards; we hear messages on the radio; we see and hear messages in various entertainment media. All of these messages convey information about what our society values. They have embedded within them implicit messages about what is desirable and undesirable, about good and bad, right and wrong. The value messages are often subtle and implied, but they are no less powerful as a result.

For example, a study conducted by *TV Guide* revealed that ninety-four percent of the sexual encounters depicted in daytime TV soap operas were between people who were not married to one another. The implied message is that sexual relations outside the context of marriage are the norm. The fact, in this particular example, that only six percent of sexual relations involved people married to one another implied a standard of behavior. This is a very subtle yet powerful value message about sexual behavior—subtle because no one is directly advocating or preaching to the viewer that sexual activity should be predominantly pursued outside of marriage. But the implied message is clear in the numbers: ninety-four percent to six percent.

Cultural value messages, of course, are not restricted to television. They can even be seen in the way we design our cities and buildings. The late Joseph Campbell wrote in his book, *The Power of Myth,* that you can tell a great deal about a culture's values by looking at its urban planning and architecture. The landscape of the towns and cities of the middle ages were dominated by magnificent cathedrals. This reflected the prominence of religion in the lives of the people of that age. In later centuries, the most impressive buildings were those built for political and national leaders, and they occupied the most conspicuous places. These palaces and government buildings reflected the importance and value people attached to political power.

What does our late twentieth century architecture and urban planning tell us of our cultural values? Contemporary landscapes are dominated by gleaming towers of steel and glass, dedicated to the endeavors of business and finance. More recently, architects and developers have entered into fierce competition to create the largest entertainment complexes and shopping malls. Each new structure is designed to be the biggest and most splendid of all, and visitors from all over the world are traveling by the millions to places like Disneyworld in Florida and the Mall of America in Minnesota.

In past centuries we used to call such journeys pilgrimages, and the travelers were called pilgrims. In the America of the 1990s, however, the pilgrimages are to the temples of money, entertainment, and materialism. The pilgrims are consumers.

This chapter began by explaining how the values of a large group can often be different from the values of that group's individual members. It is my belief that in American society today, profit has become such an overpowering societal value that it is causing great harm to our children. As a society, we are selling out our children for profit—but it is essential for us to remember that we are the society. When we say that society is transmitting values that are harmful to children and to the future of our country, we are talking about ourselves. Society is us. The only way for a society to change its course is for individual members to speak out and take responsibility for their part of the society's actions, and not limit their concerns to the things that have the most immediate effect on themselves and their own children.

If society is selling out our children, then we are selling out our children. We can either continue to let it happen, or we can start to change it.

CHAPTER 3

The Abandonment of America's Children

We've reviewed a few of the alarms that should make us concerned for America's children. We've begun to discuss why and how society is sacrificing our children's welfare and future for profit. We now must address another issue: the abandonment of our children to harmful influences.

We need to be aware that our children have to contend with powerful messages directed at them with sophisticated technology. Moreover, they are dealing with these messages more and more frequently on their own. While our American society of the late twentieth century is sending harmful messages to children at an increasing rate, parents are less present than ever before to protect their children or to filter the effects of these messages.

The family has fulfilled two essential roles for children since time immemorial: to protect and to socialize. It is a fact that human beings have the longest period of dependency of any living species; babies and small children are incapable of providing their own shelter, sustenance, and safety for years. They are dependent on adults for their very survival.

In like manner, children depend on adults for mental and emotional nurturing for many years. Developmental psychologists like

Jean Piaget and Erik Erikson have documented the crucial stages of psychosocial development and found that children depend on their adult caregivers to help them gain the ability to trust others and develop a sense of themselves as capable, autonomous and worthy. In the past century we have learned a great deal about the lifelong impact of these early interactions between children and parents.

In recent years, several leading child psychologists have focused their research on a dynamic called "attachment." This concept describes the close emotional connection formed in the early months of life between child and parent. Alan Sroufe and others have researched and documented the negative impact on children when this attachment relationship is absent or impaired. Children who are not able to "attach" to a parent frequently exhibit aggressive and anti-social behavior in their later childhood years, and the absence of parental role models makes them all the more subject to the influence of societal messages.

Society has always depended upon parents to socialize children about the ways of the community. Community standards of right and wrong, of acceptable and unacceptable behavior are transmitted to children through their earliest teachers, their parents. As noted earlier, the community would fill in for absent or deficient parents in the past, but teaching community standards was and still is considered to be primarily the parents' responsibility.

Among other things, parents provide children with their first lessons in trust, responsibility, reciprocity, discipline, and self-restraint. These traits are very important from the larger society's point of view, for they are essential if a free democratic society is to flourish. Without these traits present among its citizens, a society has to rely more heavily on law enforcement, coercion, and punishment to avoid anarchy and chaos.

However, many societal messages run contrary to these values. Rather than promote reciprocity, many such messages extol selfishness and cutthroat competition. Rather than promote discipline and self-restraint, these messages glorify instant gratification, violence, and a "win at all costs" attitude.

The problem is clear. Some of the personal traits and values that are essential for a free and healthy society are under attack by contrary, harmful messages that are being expressed more frequently in popular culture. The need to protect children and help mitigate the effects of these messages is greater than ever before; unfortunately, just when the need is greatest, parents are less available than ever.

The decrease in parental involvement in children's lives has two main causes. First of all, the pace of life has become so accelerated that American parents are caught in a time crunch. There is simply not enough time to attend to all the competing demands, and the demand that can suffer the most is that of time to spend with our children.

Family sociologists calculate that parents are spending forty percent less time interacting with their children today than they did in 1950. This fact carries more than a little irony when we consider all of the inventions and technological advances of the past forty-plus years that were supposed to save us time and provide us with more opportunities to be together as families.

The fact that parents have less time works to the detriment of children in a number of ways. Parents have less time to volunteer for child-related activities and less time to be involved in their children's schools. Leaders of organizations like the Girl Scouts and Boy Scouts, as well as PTA officials, talk about how difficult it is to get parent volunteers. The reason consistently given by parents for their lack of involvement is, "I just don't have time."

The hectic schedules that American parents follow also hamper their ability to get together with other parents on a regular basis. This is significant, because these informal connections not only lend support to harried parents, but also provide a good way for them to learn from others about the subtleties of the art of parenting. As overcrowded schedules limit these opportunities, parents inevitably feel more and more isolated and overwhelmed.

This lack of time for our children is of particular concern in light of recent studies completed by the Search Institute, a non-profit organization dedicated to promoting the positive development of children through scientific research and resource development. Researchers looking for factors that correlated positively with children doing well in life found parent involvement in school activities, consistent and appropriate discipline, the amount of time parents spend at home with their children, and parental monitoring of children's activities to be the most important.

These data should not come as a surprise to us when we consider the role of parenting in the protection and socialization functions discussed earlier. When supportive parental involvement is present, children get along better in life. (The Search Institute uses the term "thrivers" to describe these children.) In a society that I contend is hostile to children in many ways, parental involvement is all the more important.

The growing prevalence of dual career families has obviously had an impact on the amount of time parents have for their children. The solution, however, is not to return to the days where Dad went off to work and Mom looked after the children. Even if that were possible in today's economy, it would not be advisable. The solutions require joint participation involving both parents in a two-parent home, and for that matter, the extended community as well.

In fact, rather than lay the burden at the feet of women, I would suggest that it belongs more appropriately with the men, for fathers are on average more absent from the lives of their children than mothers are. Fred M. Hechinger, in his book *Fateful Choices:*

Healthy Youth for the Twenty-First Century, reports a startling statistic that illustrates this clearly. Adolescents in the United States spend on average only three minutes alone with their fathers each day, and fifty percent of that is spent watching TV.

Obviously, part of the reason parents have so little time to spend with their kids is the economic pressure many of them are under. Another indication of the decreased value society places on children is the shift in the United States tax code. The tax burden has shifted dramatically onto the backs of families with children relative to what it was in 1948. For example, when the I.R.S. introduced the original tax exemption for children in 1948, it was six hundred dollars. If that exemption had kept pace with inflation, it would now be approximately seven thousand dollars. The actual exemption is only $2,300. Professor Jean Bethke Elshtain of Vanderbilt University explains that a family of four at the median income level in 1948 paid .3 percent of their income in federal income taxes. By 1989 it had grown to 9.1 percent.

The second major factor in the decreased amount of time children have with their parents is the rapid increase in the number of children living with only one parent. According to the U.S. Census Bureau, thirty-three percent of all households with children in the United States are single parent families. This number continues to rise because of both the high divorce rate in the United States and the increase in the number of births to unmarried women. Our divorce rate is the highest in the Western world, and Census data tells us it is now approximately fifty percent. In 1992, 25.7 percent of all births in this country were to unmarried mothers, and the percentage of children born to unmarried women has increased by two hundred percent in the past twenty years, according to U.S. census data.

The trend toward single parent families is not changing, either— it is accelerating. It is estimated by sociologists Frank Furstenburg and Andrew Chalin in their book *Divided Families* that at the present rate of increase, sixty percent of all children born in the year 2000 will spend a part of their childhood in a single parent home.

The concern about this phenomenon need not be based on traditional moral grounds; there is a growing body of data about the effects of single parenting on children. Unfortunately, whether we want to admit it or not, there is a high correlation between the problems of children and the lack of a stable two-parent family. The study by the Search Institute found that children in single parent homes were at a greater risk on each of the twenty different factors they measured. These risk factors included: frequent alcohol use, binge drinking, daily tobacco use, illicit drug use, sexual acting out, depression, suicide, theft, vandalism, and truancy. This correlation held true for both boys and girls, across all racial and ethnic groups.

The parade of statistics about children of single parents is alarming. According to Professor Bethke Elshtain, seventy-five percent of teenage suicides occur in families where a parent is absent. Single-parent kids account for eighty percent of children in inpatient mental health units. I conducted research in 1984 to look for factors that correlated with serious teenage alcohol or drug abuse problems. The factor that had the highest correlation was what I called "the parental loss factor"—the absence of a parent through death, separation, or divorce.

In fact, parental absence affects more than psychosocial development. A 1988 government survey of seventeen thousand youngsters living apart from a biological parent found that the group was thirty percent more likely to become physically ill than children living with two parents.

The coining of a new term that has emerged in the last generation—"latch key kids"—is a manifestation of the problem. Kids are more and more on their own, and this is particularly true as they get older. A recent survey of fifty thousand American sixth graders revealed that greater than fifty percent of them spent more than two hours each day at home with no adult supervision. The de facto babysitter for many of these children became the television.

Children who are unsupervised or undersupervised are making decisions every day with little adult input. Some parents have little idea what their kids are doing, especially as they reach adolescence. One factor in the rise of younger and younger children engaging in sexual activity might be that kids are increasingly on their own in a society that encourages sexual acting out.

Children who live in crime-ridden neighborhoods often race home after school and lock the doors behind them. Some of these children live with a constant fear; others eventually join in the action on the streets. But it's not just in poor or inner city neighborhoods where the problems of undersupervised children arise; they cut across all neighborhoods and all socioeconomic classes.

The risk rates on all the factors I've mentioned is highest among children of mothers who never married. This last fact is particularly noteworthy in view of the now infamous Murphy Brown/Dan Quayle brouhaha. This debate exemplifies the discrepancy between reality and television's version of it. As most will recall, the TV character Murphy Brown eloquently defended single mothers and the choice of unmarried women to have children. The matter of choice is not what I am questioning. It is the depiction of the life of this particular unmarried mother, a popular and sympathetic television character. Reality is quite different. In fact, Professor Bethke Elshtain reports that the actual number of "Murphy Browns" in the United States (that is to say, single mothers with incomes greater than fifty thousand dollars a year) is less that one tenth of one percent of unwed mothers! Murphy Brown may have been eloquent, but her situation was anything but commonplace.

Most unwed mothers contend with a host of daunting challenges, especially financial hardship. Princeton sociologist Sara McLanahan has conducted studies showing that half the single mothers in the United States live below the poverty level. This contrasts sharply with the statistic that only ten percent of two-parent families are below that line.

The cultural messages in our popular culture often do not support the two parent family in spite of overwhelming evidence of how important it is for children. Popular magazines like *People* report on celebrity divorces as occasions for partying and merriment. Greeting card companies now sell cards that celebrate divorce. Cards of support might certainly be thoughtful and appropriate; cards of celebration, however, send a very different message.

Unwed parenthood is very much in vogue among entertainment celebrities. The April 1992 issue of *Vanity Fair* had a cover story on the baby born to Rebecca Brousaard and Jack Nicholson. The story explained how the two lived separately and how marriage was not only not discussed, but was avoided. "I don't discuss marriage much with Rebecca," explained Nicholson. "Those discussions are the very thing I'm trying to avoid. I'm after this immediate real thing."

Unfortunately, even our awareness of problems and our willingness to confront them has been transformed into a mockery of two-parent family life. A bumper sticker has recently appeared that reads: "Unspoken traditional family values: abuse, alcoholism, incest." Tragically, those things do happen in some families. But to insinuate that those are the "values" of the traditional family is to contribute to a cultural trend that undermines it.

Obviously, pointing a finger at single parents who are overwhelmingly women is the last thing we should do. That would be blaming the victim. These women are often leading quietly heroic lives, trying to do the best job of parenting they can in a difficult situation.

In fact, I think the greater challenge exists for men. Although many separated fathers are strongly involved with their children, the data on these fathers as a group is disappointing. Men are increasingly absent from families. Studies by Princeton University sociologist Sara McLanahan show that fathers of out-of-wedlock children and divorced fathers provide too little economic and emotional support. And in a recent study by Furstenburg and Cherlin, only sixteen percent of the children whose fathers did not live with them saw their fathers on a weekly basis. A full fifty percent of the children had not seen their fathers in the previous twelve months. Clearly, men have to take greater responsibility for the children they are fathering.

The underlying point being made here is that negative cultural messages about marriage and two-parent families have a real impact on our children and the adults they will become. As we have "normalized" what was previously considered a problem, we have blinded ourselves to the harmful effects on children.

Of course, this is not to say that a child in a single-parent family is condemned to the litany of problems listed earlier; there are many such children doing a great deal better than their counterparts in two-parent families. But we do need to acknowledge that in most cases, being a child of a single parent puts that child at greater risk. By breaking through our denial we will be better able to support single parents. Moreover, we need to start challenging the cultural messages that contribute to divorce and unwanted pregnancy.

Another discrepancy between media images and reality relates to blended families. The TV versions are often cute and humorous. In workshop after workshop on blended families I have facilitated, however, parents tell me that the challenges were much greater than they ever anticipated. They also were clear that their personal experiences and media portrayals of blended families were very, very different.

We adults have gotten ourselves into a situation where our children are being neglected. Moreover, through the messages our society sends us, we too often try to deny the seriousness of the problem. I think we need to consider suggestions like the following to reverse the situation:

First of all, I believe we need to work for changes in government and industry policy that make children a priority. For instance, we should try to help parents remain at home for extended periods after childbirth. The fact that seventy percent of women are afraid to tell their bosses that they are pregnant says a great deal about our society's attitude toward children and the importance of family. The recent passage of the Family Leave Act was a step in the right direction, but more needs to be done.

I am aware of the economic costs of such a suggestion, but I don't think we have any choice in view of the way things are going. It's too often shallow rhetoric when we say that our children are our most important investment. We have to start to act like we mean it.

This carries over to revisions of the tax code to give parents some relief. We need to realize they'll make up any loss in revenue when they're finished parenting. And if we raise productive citizens, they'll be contributing to the national treasury as well.

The examples of children who thrive can lead us to other improvements we can make. We need to get more involved in our children's schools. We need to supervise and monitor our children's activities. We need to provide firm, appropriate, and loving discipline. Of course, we can only do that if we're there.

Let me reiterate that these suggestions, while intended for all parents, are particularly important for men. This is because the data suggests that we fathers spend less time with our kids than mothers.

I also believe we need to reexamine and challenge cultural messages about marriage, two-parent families, and sexuality.

All of this really boils down to priorities. We must reorient our priorities if our nation's children are to thrive. This will require a great deal of commitment and sacrifice. Unfortunately, sacrifice is not one of our society's cherished values anymore. But we can make changes on a personal level, and in so doing, change our society.

CHAPTER 4

The Power of Advertising

Nike, Starter, Reebok . . . Do these names sound familiar? They are household words across the country, conjuring up images of speed, power, status, and perfection for many American children. For any parent trying to stick to a household budget, these words may also bring to mind arguments with children in a shoe store over a one-hundred-dollar pair of sneakers.

If we as parents won't fork over the money, then our children may reach into their own pockets and buy the shoes with wages from their part-time jobs. In other cases, guns or knives are used by kids to get these coveted possessions. The killing of someone for their sneakers is not an isolated incident anymore.

What has endowed these shoes with such power that they are worth killing for? Advertising! In order to comprehend the value children place on certain consumer goods, we need to understand the tremendous power of society's most influential kind of communication.

The science of advertising has evolved a great deal during the past century. Psychologists, demographers, artists, writers, marketers and business leaders collaborate to create messages expressly intended to shape our opinions and change our behavior. After all, advertisers are in the business of persuasion.

Today, advertising is very directly involved in the formation of cultural values. If I can be motivated to value a product or service, I can be motivated to acquire it, which is the advertiser's goal. Therefore, advertising must be as effective as possible in shaping values.

Let's look at a common example. An advertisement for a pair of jeans has one goal: to get me to purchase that brand of jeans. To accomplish this, the advertisers have to get inside my head and make me want to buy their brand. That's not an easy task. Getting someone to want to buy something involves persuading them to value it. I have to believe that the brand is better for me in some way. I have to see it as having a positive value.

A great deal of money, energy, and talent has been dedicated to honing this science of persuasion, and the results are quite impressive. Advertising has become very effective in shaping values and influencing behavior.

Anyone who doubts the power of advertising should go back and analyze some of the most recent U.S. election campaigns. Quick-hitting, extremely superficial political advertising has greatly affected the outcome of elections, and by extension, the direction of this country. And if advertising can persuade people to cast votes, it is no surprise that it is extremely effective in persuading us to buy things, believe claims, and behave in ways beneficial to those responsible for that advertising. As a shaper of opinions, beliefs, and behavior, advertising is a major social force.

The psychology of modern advertising is based on some rather simple but very powerful principles. Advertisers attempt to create a specific emotional state in the viewer or listener that will make that person receptive to their message. They might do this through humor, pleasant or frightening imagery, appealing or dramatic music, or the presence of a popular celebrity. When that mood or emotional state has been created, the advertiser injects a message about a product or a service. That service or product is then linked to those feelings, whether as a means to achieve pleasant experiences or as a way to avoid unpleasant ones. In this way, the person exposed to the advertisement is drawn to the product. The more sophisticated the ad, the more likely it is that this linkage will happen on an unconscious level.

Advertisers are adept at manipulating a variety of emotions to generate motivation to change behavior. They may elicit a fear response in us, for example, with threatening or scary scenes. After that emotion has been stimulated, then relief will be associated with their product. Or advertisers may stimulate our greed with messages and images connected to get-rich-quick schemes. Advertisers can augment these techniques with music, rhyme and repetition to promote greater retention of product names.

Although these principles are not terribly complex, they are extremely effective in shaping the opinions and behavior of millions upon millions of people. With advances in media technology, emotional states are more effectively created, and linkages are more strongly formed than ever before. Millions of Americans are able to repeat advertising slogans or jingles from memory without ever consciously trying to memorize them. The game "Adverteasing" is a testimony to the effectiveness of advertiser's efforts. It consists of twenty-one hundred slogans, commercials, or jingles that are read aloud. The object of the game is to identify the associated product. Players are often amazed at the recall they have about products promoted decades ago.

See if you can complete the following sentence: "Winston tastes good like a..." It is likely that you can complete the sentence even though it may have been a matter of decades since you heard it last. The jingle "Winston tastes good like a cigarette should" was so well communicated that millions still remember it.

In this country, the power of the psychology of persuasion has been focused on the promotion of consumerism for the past seventy years. It was in the 1920s and 1930s, however, that mass production led to sophisticated advertising techniques that promote the notion of replacing goods out of a desire for something new rather than to replace something that has worn out.

This was the era when radio came into its own as a mass medium. It quickly became a vehicle for carrying commercial messages into homes in ways and styles that were completely new. Products literally had their praises sung in the living rooms of target audiences. Newly-created radio celebrities talked persuasively about their sponsor's products to listeners in the manner of one friend talking to another. It was one thing to see a celebrity's picture with an endorsed product in a print ad; it was quite another thing to have that celebrity talking to you in your own home. Whether it was Bing Crosby for Primo Cigars, Edgar Bergen and Charley McCarthy for Chase and Sanborn Coffee, or a fictional character such as Jack Armstrong, the all-American boy, touting Wheaties, the novelty of radio and the audience loyalty it created was a perfect vehicle for selling things.

The onset of World War II slowed down the booming consumerism for a time. Raw materials were needed for the production of war implements and supplies, so conservation became a mark of patriotism. Americans were called upon to make sacrifices of every sort to support the national effort.

Once the war ended, however, the juggernaut of consumerism gathered momentum. First of all, there was pent-up demand for consumer products after the period of scarcity during the war. Secondly, skyrocketing birthrates in the postwar baby boom and the rapid growth of suburban communities meant rapidly expanding target markets. Thirdly, there was a new and very potent medium available for advertising messages: television.

Television proved to be an even more effective medium for communication than radio because it appealed to the visual and auditory senses simultaneously. Celebrities could now be seen as well as heard in America's homes as they helped to promote this product or that.

For the past forty years since the inception of television, techniques to promote the purchase of more and more products have been refined and have become increasingly effective. Obsolescence was built into products so that replacements would be needed in a short time. Yearly unveilings of new models are now ritualized for a broad array of goods, from clothing to automobiles to household appliances. The goal is to convince people that the old is inferior in order to entice them to buy the new.

In order to maintain growth in consumer product industries, people have to purchase more and more. To encourage this, messages have been communicated through advertising to increase consumer motivation to buy. One type of message links status to products. The message is, "If you want to be a somebody you have to have _____." Twenty years ago, fashion designers began to pretentiously affix their labels to the outside of clothing so other people would know at a glance the status of the person wearing it. This tactic produced a "mine is better than yours" mentality and fueled increased purchasing.

Newer and more subtle avenues for advertising continue to be discovered. The film industry now enters into product placement contracts. Manufacturers and distributors are offered the opportunity to buy visibility in movies. For a sum of money, they are guaranteed that their products will be used by characters or will be prominently placed on the sets. The particular box of cereal on the breakfast table or the specific delivery truck on the street did not get into the movie by accident. Advertisers have found another avenue to motivate us to buy without us knowing that we are watching a paid advertisement.

Lately, television has been broadcasting more and more "infomercials." These are thirty minute advertisements masquerading as entertainment programs or as documentaries.

The search for new ways to get our attention is unrelenting. A recent controversy involves televised sports. A few teams have begun selling advertising space behind home plate during baseball games, knowing the TV cameras won't be able to avoid broadcasting it. Also, cigarette companies have been accused of buying space at ballparks for the same reason, as a way of circumventing the ban on television ads for cigarettes. Some stadiums have adopted a policy against selling space to them, but many others have not.

Product identification with movies and television is not new. In the 1950s, kids purchased Davy Crockett caps in droves after seeing their hero on the screen. Mickey Mouse paraphernalia has been sold for decades. It has simply evolved into a more precise science, and become much more subtle in some cases.

All around us, different forms of this merchandising abound. Sensing big profits, companies transform movies like Jurassic Park and The Terminator into computer games. Breakfast cereals, fast food restaurants, and t-shirts bear the logos of an immense variety of products. Many Saturday morning cartoons have become thinly disguised vehicles for product promotion. (And it doesn't stop there—the cartoons are shown after school, too, and new cartoons are rarely launched without a toy tie-in.)

The messages of advertisers are everywhere. From the moment we wake up in the morning until the moment we fall asleep at night, we are bombarded with thousands of their messages. They jump off the wrappers of food items. They scream at us over the radio waves. We see them on massive billboards as we drive along our highways. This is not only the world we live in; this is the world our children live in.

Every single one of these advertising messages is the product of a great deal of thought, planning, and execution. Every single one is intended to get our attention and to change our behavior. If ads were not effective, the advertising industry would not pay such enormous sums of money to get their messages in front of us. A thirty second spot during the 1994 Super Bowl cost nine hundred thousand dollars. Why did advertisers pay it? Because they knew it was worth the money.

Now that we have discussed how advertising works and how powerful it is, we need to ask ourselves toward what ends this powerful technology is directed. The answer can be found in a quote from B. Earl Puckett, the former president of Allied Stores, a large conglomerate of department stores: "It is our job to make people unhappy with what they have." Although this statement was listed as a casual tidbit type of filler in a Sunday newspaper magazine, it speaks volumes about the goals of advertisers with products and services to sell.

When clever advertising aimed at making us unhappy with what we have is focused on young customers—children who are just forming their own self-image and self-esteem—then the effect of manipulative commercials is all the more powerful. The results are frantic rock-music-driven ads that engulf children with the message to "get it now!"

Zeroing In On Kids

Advertisers are increasingly targeting children with their technologies of persuasion. This is partly because they learned a very important lesson in the recession of 1991. During that year, advertising revenues plummeted. Many magazines went out of business. Radio and television sales forces had difficulty selling their "spots." But during this period there was one bright spot: children's television programs sold out. During this bleak year for advertisers, the children's market stood out as the lone beacon of hope.

The reasons for this were twofold. The first was the size of the children's market. The second was its growing influence.

The children's market is still growing, both demographically and in purchasing power. According to U.S. Census Bureau projections, the population of children is projected to increase during the next twelve years, and there will be a bulge in the teenage population. This fact is not lost on advertisers.

The television show *Beverly Hills 90210* is a good example. It generally scores low in overall ratings, but stays on the air because of the viewer demographics—all teens and preteens. Advertisers who want to reach these kids are willing to buy commercial time even though the overall ratings are not as high as those of other shows.

Even more significant than the demographic growth of children, however, is the increase in their purchasing power. In 1994, it is estimated that youth in the United States age three to seventeen will actually spend 50.4 billion dollars, according to *American Demographics* magazine. As we saw in the previous chapter, children are more and more on their own; consequently, they make more and more of their own purchasing decisions.

With less time for their children, parents are increasingly likely to give them money to buy things, both because they don't have time to supervise their choices and because they want to keep their children occupied. Kids, as a result, control a bigger and bigger slice of the family financial pie.

The infamous bank robber of the 50s, Willie Sutton, was once asked why he kept robbing banks. His quick and simple reply is well known: "Because that's where the money is." Advertisers know where the money is, too—in the hands of our children.

We have noted the purchasing power of kids when it comes to products for their exclusive use and entertainment. Marketers and advertisers have also become aware of another phenomenon of the marketplace: as parents have become busier, more decisions about purchases of household goods are being formally and informally delegated to their children. Children are being asked to pick up items for meals or other household needs, and children are accompanying parents on quick stops at the store on the way home from daycare or school. The result is that children are exerting a greater and greater influence on household buying decisions. The purchasing influence of children age three to seventeen in the United States is now estimated to be three hundred and forty billion dollars a year. These estimates were calculated by James McNeal, a Texas A & M Professor, who has studied kids' marketing for twenty-five years. While children's purchases are still mainly for personal entertainment items, their purchasing influence is increasingly extending well into the choice of products and services not traditionally considered in their domain.

As the economic muscle of children grows, the advertising industry is paying much greater attention to them. The messages aimed at kids are much more technologically sophisticated than ever before, and there is also much greater segmentation of the children's market. The Nielsen Media Research organization, for example, continues to produce more data on the children's market, breaking down the viewership of programs into very specific age groups. Preschoolers are differentiated from grade school kids, who are in turn differentiated from teens.

In doing research for this section of the book, I had both a fascinating and at the same time frightening experience. To learn about how advertisers look at children, I found myself immersed in journals that I had never read before. They were the professional trade publications of the marketers and advertisers. Not belonging to that profession, I had never before taken the time to read extensively in this area.

I learned some fascinating things in the process. For example, I learned in *American Demographics* magazine that advertisers believe that a child becomes a consumer at age three. I also learned how an advertising campaign aimed at children gets coordinated; a very successful marketer of video games described how she uses television to pique kids' interest in her products. That phase, she said, is carefully followed up by a magazine campaign aimed at really "hooking the kids." How many adults know that *Boy's Life* magazine is read by five million boys a month? I didn't—but the marketers of video games do.

I also learned of the enormous sums of money advertisers spend to reach our children's minds. Professor McNeal reported that in 1992, 6.8 billion dollars was targeted at the four to twelve age group alone. When we realize that advertisers use those kinds of financial resources to promote products, the profits to be made in marketing to children are put in a startling perspective.

The most frightening part for me, however, was when I paired this information about advertising strategies with the data I had gleaned from other sources about the products being advertised. For instance, a study done in 1989 by the National Coalition on Television Violence found that eighty percent of Nintendo video games sold in the United States have violence as a theme.

The Bottom Line

The important thing to remember in this discussion is not any specific fact or figure. It is the realization that all of this effort and expense is aimed at children as consumers, not learners. In the world of marketing and advertising, children are targeted for profit, not education.

As we've seen, advertising is in the business of influencing behavior. It has developed sophisticated and powerful technologies, and is capable of shaping values and changing how we view things. In our anonymous society, however, the cutting edge of that technology is usually not employed to teach right from wrong, to increase children's self-esteem, or to strengthen values of cooperation, respect, responsibility, and hard work. It is used to maximize profit. If positive values are reinforced in the process, fine. If they are undermined in the process, however, then that's just too bad. As the character Gordon Gekko says in the movie *Wall Street:* "It's all about bucks, kid. The rest is conversation."

CHAPTER 5

Television

"All television is educational. The question is, what does it teach?" This statement by Nicholas Johnson, the former head of the Federal Communications Commission, points to the enormous influence television has on today's children. Any discussion of society's values and the transmission of those values must include an examination of television, which is one of society's most powerful voices.

Since the beginning of humankind, children have learned skills and values by watching adults. Young children, for example, develop language by imitating their parents. We have recently learned that children start this imitating even earlier than we had previously suspected. Children are like sponges in their ability to absorb learning, literally from the moment of birth. Some say learning begins even earlier, during fetal development.

We have always known that children are keen observers. With limited experience, they rely on modeling to learn how to function in the world. Whether it's a matter of learning how to speak or how to catch a baseball, they do it by observing others and trying to imitate the skill themselves.

Children acquire values in the same manner. By observation, imitation, and trial and error interactions, they gradually learn what is important in life and what is unimportant, what is valued and what isn't. The dramatic play of children is a clear example of this phenomenon at work. Children literally "try out" adult behavior by putting on adult clothes and imitating the behavior they have observed.

For thousands of years, that pattern of observation and imitation happened directly between parents and children. When most people lived in small villages or tribes, the adults were constantly around for children to observe. When they were old enough and had learned from their parents through observation, they could take part in adult activities themselves. Until they reached the appropriate age, however, they would play-act with their peers.

About two hundred and fifty years ago, at the time of the Industrial Revolution, this learning process began to change dramatically. As the production of goods shifted from home and village to factories, large numbers of workers were brought together. This changed not only how products were made, but also altered how society organized itself. Large numbers of people moved from rural areas to urban centers so they could have jobs and support themselves. The growth of cities brought still other changes, especially in the way children learned.

The opportunity for children to learn directly from adults was lessened. Adults working in factories were not around children as much, so just as factories brought the adults together to work, another institution—schools—evolved to bring children together to learn. Children learned from other designated adults: teachers.

Schools began to share in the function of parenting. They received the societal mandate to educate children in skills and to assist parents in the important job of passing on society's values. As the Industrial Revolution took hold, parents and schools increasingly shared child-rearing responsibilities.

Children, as a result of this profound societal change, began to divide their time between family and school. They were still learning by observing and imitating, but now they were doing it in the context of two major social institutions: the family and the school.

Beginning around 1950, however, another significant change occurred. Its impact on children's learning was as great as the social changes brought about by the Industrial Revolution, if not more so. That change was the introduction of television. Another major teacher entered the lives of children, and this time it was an electronic teacher.

The rapid growth of television was phenomenal. In 1950, only ten percent of American families had a television set in their homes. By the end of the decade that percentage had skyrocketed to ninety percent. Not only were the number of televisions increasing; the amount of time children spent watching them grew as well. From the earliest days of programming, shows were specifically targeted to children. Programs like *Howdy Doody* and *Captain Video* began almost immediately.

The decade of the 1980s brought additional changes. During those years, cable television, video cassette recorders, and interactive video games were introduced to many Americans, and they quickly began to appear in more and more homes. These developments dramatically increased the impact television had on children's lives and activities. In fact, studies show that the total number of hours spent watching television and playing video games now approaches thirty-five hours a week for the average American child. Cable television and VCRs not only affect the amount of time kids spend watching, but also have made significant changes in what they are watching. VCRs let kids watch late night programming that wasn't intended for them. They also mean that kids never have to miss a program—they can simply record it for later viewing. Cable television has greatly expanded the number of choices, and has provided access to "adult entertainment."

All this is evidence of the fact that in the past forty years, television has assumed a dominant role in the lives of America's children. (Not surprising when you keep in mind that the TV set is usually positioned in the most prominent place in the home.) Consider the following: There are 168 hours in a week. Assuming a child sleeps eight to ten hours at night, that leaves between 98 and 112 waking hours. About thirty of those hours are spent at school, and another ten are spent traveling to and from various places. If we subtract another ten for personal care needs like dressing, and bathing, we are left with between forty-eight and sixty-two hours for all other activities. These would include play, homework, meals, chores, and socializing with friends and family. However, the statistics tell us that the majority of that time is now spent in front of one television screen or another. In fact, the amount of time spent in front of a television or video screen is the single biggest chunk of time in the waking life of an average American child.

We discussed earlier in this chapter how children learn by watching their world and imitating the behavior they observe. Beginning in 1950, that window on the world has increasingly been the television screen. Children now spend more time learning about life through television than in any other manner.

Television is not only the prominent teacher of today's youth; it is also powerfully attractive to kids. Any parent who has tried to get the attention of a child watching a program knows how hypnotic it can be. Parents I meet complain that a bomb could go off, and if their kids were watching TV or playing Nintendo, they would be oblivious to it. The combination of the visual with the auditory seems to be the ingredient that makes television and videos so much more attractive than other media like books or radio.

Traditionally, family, church, and school have been the primary influences on a child's intellectual, emotional, and moral development. That is no longer the case. In terms of time spent, the biggest influence is now the television set. What's even more disturbing is that its influence is growing, extending into other parts of our children's lives.

Television is no longer relegated to the home—it has recently invaded the school as well. Channel One is a company that has approached schools with an offer too good for many of them to pass up. It goes like this: Channel One offers to equip entire schools with televisions in every classroom, at no expense to the school. Furthermore, they will produce and transmit high quality educational programs to the schools. Once again, this is at no cost to the institution. There's only one catch. To take advantage of this great deal, the school has to agree not to turn off the set during the commercials.

So now, even schools are no longer a safe haven for children from the commercial messages of television. The schools who sign up are willing partners in extending the influence of television into the lives of children. These schools become unwitting co-conspirators in the effort to exploit children as consumers and a source of profit.

Schools and school districts are signing on in droves. The motivation is financial. The lure of free television sets and free programming is very appealing to administrators straining to spread limited funds as far as possible. As one administrator of a private high school put it, "It's too good of a financial deal to pass up."

A Window On The World

In the 1990s, kids are doing what kids have always done. They are learning about the world and about life by observing. They are developing values by seeing them modeled and reinforced. What has changed, however, is that children are not imitating and modeling adults who are solely interested in their growth and development. Children are not always taught by those who want to teach them right from wrong. Rather, observation and learning is taking place for many hours of the day in front of a television set. And most of what is shown has one purpose: to make money.

Television is a business. Broadcast TV is paid for by advertisers who have products and services to sell. The more people watch certain programs (in other words, the higher the ratings) the more money the television companies can charge for commercial time. (In the case of pay cable channels, higher viewership means that there is more demand, so they can raise their subscription fees.) The more money television companies can charge, the higher their profits will be. Everyone in this cycle is pleased with higher ratings, since advertisers want their messages to reach as big an audience as possible, "target marketing" notwithstanding.

Even public television is part of this business, although certainly less so than its commercial counterparts. Extensive merchandising campaigns are linked to PBS shows like *Sesame Street* and *Barney*. And viewers have noticed that corporate donations are announced in ways that are becoming more and more like commercials. These "benevolent" corporations carefully choose which shows to "support." *This Old House*, for example, is usually supported by paint, window, and hardware manufacturers.

Because the name of the game is profit, television networks and production companies will do whatever they can to increase their share of the market. Television, therefore, has become our marketing tool. The goal of television is to capture the public's attention and hold it long enough so the advertisers who are paying the bill can sell a product.

If people didn't get the advertisers' messages, the whole business of television would collapse. So the stations have to get people to pay attention in order to give the advertisers their opportunity to sell. However, it's not easy to catch someone's attention and hold it. It is particularly challenging when the target audience has become progressively desensitized because of constant exposure to television programming.

If I am going to grab and keep your attention, I have to do something to arouse you emotionally. Consequently, television producers try to arouse powerful emotions in us to get our attention. Certain things arouse emotions more reliably than others. Among the most reliable are violence, sex, and humor. Violence stimulates the adrenal glands and arouses us. Sexually oriented material stimulates and arouses us. Humor arouses us as well with changes in brain chemistry we have yet to completely decipher.

It is not surprising, therefore, that the major themes of television entertainment are violence, sex, and humor. Not information or education, although there are some exceptions. For the most part, TV sticks to the themes that sell, because selling things is what television is all about.

Every moment of television entertainment has to be arousing. As a result, programming is increasingly fast-paced. As children watch more and more TV, the machine gun pace becomes essential to keep them involved, which explains why shows aimed at youth are so often frenetic. Many adults cannot watch MTV, for example, because it produces a sensory overload. They complain that it's too loud, too fast, too chaotic, too sexual. This might be true for adults, but not for a generation of kids who are being raised on it.

Even serious and informational adult programs like television news have changed to include more elements of violence, sex, and humor, and to maintain a faster pace. Ratings wars among news programs are very intense, and news programs are becoming increasingly sensational and fast-paced to capture the audience's attention. In-depth reporting on any one subject is becoming a rarity as the five-second "sound byte" becomes the norm.

Why has television become a major teacher of children and a major shaper of values? Because of the way children learn and because of how much time they spend watching it. The goal of television, however, is rarely to educate or to shape values. The goal, as we have seen, is to sell things. Therefore, values that are good for children are not the guiding principles for TV. The marketplace provides TV's guiding principles.

Our society has developed an extremely powerful teacher, but the teacher has only the values of the marketplace driving it. And the value messages of the marketplace are increasingly at odds with those values that are important for healthy children and a healthy society.

The Values Espoused By Television

Since television is so influential, we should be aware of the values it is promoting. What are the value messages our children are picking up from TV?

1) Violence Despite what we say about the evil of violence, it is promoted as exciting and glamorous on television. It is often portrayed as the solution to fictional characters' problems. According to the National Coalition on Television Violence, the average child in the United States will witness over two hundred thousand acts of violence on television by the time he or she is eighteen years old. As we've discussed, acts of violence stimulate an emotional response, which is why television uses it for entertainment. (The issue of violence and children will be explored at greater length in the next chapter.)

2) Sex The average child in the United States will receive about forty-five thousand messages about sex from television during their formative years, according to a TV Guide study. In an example mentioned previously, sexual encounters on TV soap operas take place between unmarried people ninety-four percent of the time. On prime time television, references to sexual activity are generally between unmarried people as well. In addition, sexual activity is often presented in a light, humorous context. It was very prominent in the most popular shows watched by a sample of eleven hundred ten to fourteen year olds in a study done in 1986 and reported by Cornell University Family Studies professor John Condry.

As mentioned earlier, sex is so prevalent on television because it elicits a strong viewer response, which is precisely the goal of the program producers. These strong responses catch our attention and lead to higher ratings.

3) **Wealth** According to what kids see on television, the key to happiness is money and the material possessions it buys. They not only get this message in commercials, but in the content of the programs themselves. The economic status of television characters and families generally far exceeds that of typical Americans.

Wealth is valued on television because it elicits a response of desire or longing on the part of the viewer. Who among us doesn't like nice things and the accouterments of an affluent lifestyle? In addition, these images are a great reinforcement for the commercial messages that teach that happiness is equated with having things.

4) **Rewards Without Work** In spite of the affluence of television characters, we hardly ever see them working. The connection between work and reward is almost nonexistent. An example from the late 80s was one of the most popular shows on television—The Cosby Show. While the show was highly regarded by many educators because of its portrayal of healthy parenting, there was a nagging question for many adult viewers. The main character, played by Bill Cosby, was an obstetrician. Many people wondered how someone who made a living as an obstetrician could work so little. Physician friends of mine expressed irrita-

tion that the lifestyle portrayed in the show was so different from that of real life.

5) **Drugs and Alcohol** Cornell Professor John Condry did an interesting but alarming study in 1989 regarding television messages about drugs and alcohol. In sampling thirty-six hours of television, he identified 149 drug/alcohol related messages. A message was rated as pro-drug or alcohol if the scene portrayed the usage in a positive light, and anti-drug or alcohol if it portrayed it in a negative light. Of the 149 messages, 121 were pro drug/alcohol and only 22 were negative portrayals. The overall pro drug ratio of six to one climbed to ten to one when restricted to alcohol alone. The official government campaign regarding drugs was "just say no." However, that message was drowned out on television by a six to one margin of "just say yes" messages.

6) **Selfishness** The work and analysis of John Condry also provided insight into the premium put on selfishness. He found that individual happiness is emphasized in nearly sixty percent of TV commercials, more than double of any other value. Commercials aimed at kids stressed having fun and hardly ever mentioned social values like being helpful or being concerned for others. Selfishness is encouraged in television commercials because it prompts us to acquire things for ourselves, which is the goal of the advertiser.

7) **Disrespect** Television (and increasingly radio) glorifies an "in your face" approach to relationships. Aggression and disrespect are portrayed as humorous and attractive. The MTV creation, *Beavis and Butthead,* brought this to a new depth. The very popular show revolves around the exploits of two cartoon characters who torture animals, harass girls, and sniff paint thinner. Defenders of the show defend it as "satire." This argument is hard to accept, however, when we consider that it appeals to and is targeted at the young audience it depicts. Here's a sample of an actual line of

dialogue: "Hey Beavis, let's go over to Stuart's house and light one in his cat's butt."

After a tragic "copycat" fire claimed the life of a young girl, the producers made a concession to outraged parents and officials. They agreed that in future episodes, Beavis and Butthead would refrain from setting fires for fun.

In fairness, we must remember that every generation has had its much-admired disrespectful child figures. Dennis the Menace, The Little Rascals, and Alvin the Chipmunk are well-known examples. Young children find such characters attractive because they can vicariously "tweak" adults and get away with it. However, there is a big difference between mischievous characters and sociopathic ones.

The Effects Of Television's Value Messages

The effects of all of these messages are pervasive and extensive, and the volume of studies documenting their harmful effects is growing. A 1990 study published by the American Academy of Pediatricians demonstrated the correlation between twenty-five hours per week of television viewing with aggressive behavior, childhood obesity, and sleep disturbances.

Drs. Jerome and Dorothy Singer have spent the past twenty years studying the effects of television on children's development. These two researchers at Yale University have discovered that children who watch the most television tend to be less imaginative, more restless, more aggressive, and have poorer concentration.

Finally, a Penn State University medical school study published in 1993 documented the link between aggressive and disobedient behavior of children and the number of hours spent watching TV. The more TV the children watched, the more aggressive and impulsive they were.

These studies are but a sample among hundreds that document the effects of television on America's kids. (Many people aren't aware of these studies because they rely on television for their information, and the television industry is not highly motivated to tell this story to the American public.)

We really shouldn't be surprised to learn of TV's negative impact on values. As was pointed out earlier, kids will learn what they're taught, and television is a powerful teacher. But it's a teacher by accident—its main goal is to make money. And money is a powerful motivating force when it comes to industry resistance against reform.

An example of the television industry's response to efforts aimed at increasing the quality of children's television can be seen in its reaction to the Children's Television Act of 1990. This legislation required stations to carry informational and educational shows in their lineup. Instead of developing new shows aimed at children's needs, however, old cartoons and sitcoms were repackaged with new "educational" labels. For instance, it was claimed that the old cartoon *The Jetsons* was supposed to prepare kids for life in the next century. The show *Teenage Mutant Ninja Turtles* was actually claimed as a kind of animal documentary.

Whether or not a show is appropriate or good for children is secondary at best for most producers and TV stations. They're paid to create and broadcast shows that make money, so the people who bring us television don't have the incentive to develop shows that will help children grow emotionally or cognitively. Instead they're encouraged to develop programs that raise viewership. If violence and explicit sex raise viewership, then they will test the bounds of the FCC's Standards and Practices guidelines to deliver it.

The industry leaders defend themselves by saying that they are simply giving the American public what it wants. They further argue that if parents don't want their children to watch certain programs, then they should not permit them to do so. It becomes a circular argument. The industry blames parents and parents blame the industry. Both need to take responsibility.

In support of the industry's arguments, one factor is that many children are unsupervised for long periods of time and therefore can tune in whatever they choose. Another is that some parents are unaware of the impact of television and therefore do not monitor it adequately. Yet a third factor is that some parents are negligent in their responsibility to manage their children's viewing habits. But does that give the television and video industry free license to broadcast whatever will sell?

According to the Federal Communications Commission, the public owns the airwaves, which are in turn leased to the networks to serve the public. As broadcast commentator Susan Berkson asks, "Is serving children a steady diet of violence, sadism, psychopaths, rape, and mayhem 'serving the public?'"

Many children do want to see violence and adult shows. Many children also want to eat a lot of ice cream and no vegetables. We wouldn't dream of letting them exist on an ice cream diet, because it is not good for them—they would not develop healthy bodies and would suffer from malnutrition. Yet many of us let our children watch a steady diet of television shows that are not good for their emotional development. The people who produce and broadcast TV programming and commercials don't have an incentive to care. Parents should.

What Can We Do?

Forbidding children to watch TV altogether is ill-advised, for three reasons: First, it's unrealistic. TV is too much a part of the fabric of our culture. Second, prohibiting the use of television merely increases its attraction as forbidden fruit. Third, banning television eliminates the legitimate and worthwhile benefits it can provide. There are some excellent shows on TV.

Our goal should be to help our children learn how to use television appropriately. Here are some suggestions for parents:

1. Avoid using television as a babysitter. It might be convenient for busy parents, but it can often begin a pattern of indiscriminate viewing. If children are in a daycare setting, parents should make sure the kids are not plunked in front of a TV as a substitute for games or other activities.

2. Limit the use of TV. While some television shows may not espouse the harmful messages we've discussed, children can still suffer from spending too many hours of TV watching. Its use needs to be limited—and that means turning it off a lot more frequently than we do now.

3. Watch TV together. When the television is on, it is very helpful to watch it—at least some of the time—with our children. This enables parents to be aware of the things their kids are experiencing and the messages they are seeing and hearing. More importantly, it gives parents a chance to talk about the programs and advertisements—parents and children can discuss the values involved. These can be some very teachable moments.

By viewing together, parents can also help children understand the techniques of advertising as it tries to manipulate us to buy more and more. Finally, parents gain the opportunity to discuss with children how individuals and families on TV compare with those of the real world.

4. Examine how you use television yourself. The example we set will have a lot of influence on the viewing habits of our kids. We need to ask ourselves if we have the set on all the time, or if we watch reruns of shows we've already seen. Do we "channel surf" just to pass time? We need to make sure that there is a program on worth watching and that we don't just turn the set on at random.

5. Establish some clear ground rules. Examples include no TV before school, during daytime hours, during meals, or before homework is done.

6. Use the VCR to your advantage. Tape a commercial show and play it back later. This allows for fast forwarding through commercials and lessens their impact. It can also reduce the amount of time spent watching TV, since a half hour show can be seen in its entirety in about twenty-three minutes when you zip through the commercials.

7. Do not give the television the most prominent location in the house. Research shows that people watch less TV if it's not the focal point of activity.

8. Keep television sets out of kids' rooms. Putting them there encourages more viewing and diminishes a parent's ability to monitor their use.

9. Make sure you know what a movie or video is about and what it's rated before you give permission to view it. This includes what is seen at friends' houses, too. Make it clear to your kids that they are not allowed to view PG or R-rated movies without clearing them with you first.

10. Use the radio, records, or tapes when the television is not on. Help kids realize that other forms of media are enjoyable too.

11. Provide alternative activities that are enjoyable. Simply turning the set off is not nearly as effective as planning some other fun activity with the entire family. That way your kids won't simply be sitting around sulking over not being able to watch.

Imagine for a minute the following scene: The doorbell rings at your home, and you get up to answer it. The guest at the door asks if he can come into your home for awhile to talk to your children. You agree, and invite your children into the living room. This guest then proceeds to persuade them to accept values by exhorting, cajoling, and mesmerizing them. The problem is, the values being promoted are ones you disagree with.

What would you do? All the parents I've talked to say they would usher this guest right out the door.

Well, every family in the United States has such a guest in their home, and this guest is much more persuasive and slick than anyone who might come ringing the doorbell. Furthermore, most of us don't even think about the value messages of this guest, the television. It's time we paid attention to the guest in our home who is teaching our children.

CHAPTER 6

The Promotion of Violence

A man walks toward you. You raise your gun and shoot. He falls to the ground gasping, crying, trying to crawl away. You shoot again, but he's not dead yet. So you aim more carefully this time and squeeze the trigger. You hear the bullet whine. The man's face betrays pain and terror as his body convulses violently. Suddenly he is still, finally dead.

A scene from a bad dream? No, this is a scene from an interactive arcade video game titled "Mad Dog McCree." Complete with large screen video, high volume sound effects, and lifelike weapons, children anxiously await their turn in line so they can try their skill at simulated murder. The revenues from this game reached nine million dollars in 1991 and placed it among the top money-making video arcade games in the U.S.

Both in video arcades and in our living rooms, America's children are fed a steady diet of increasingly graphic and violent entertainment. Ultraviolent video games are one of the most glaring examples of the exploitation of children for profit. They also represent one of the most dramatic clashes in values between what is healthy for our children and our society and what our society will allow in the name of making money.

One of the cornerstones of any civilized society is the ability of its members to get along reasonably well and to peacefully resolve differences and conflicts. While that value is necessary for the survival of a democracy, and while it is a value embraced by an overwhelming majority of parents and families, it is not a value of the larger, anonymous society we live in.

The contradictions are painfully obvious: As the nation's concern about violence grows every day, the rate of reported crime in the United States is the highest in the industrialized world. Many of us would never consider vacationing in Northern Ireland because it is perceived to be a dangerous place, but the reality is that the murder rate in Northern Ireland is only half of what it is in our own country. We have a higher percentage of our population in prison than in the former Soviet Union or in South Africa. The violent crime rate among fifteen-year-old males in the U.S. is increasing by thirty-six percent a year, according to a study conducted by the National Crime Analysis Project at Northeastern University.

As our fear of violent crime worsens, leaders from every walk of life speak out. Educators, politicians, physicians, clergy, and parents all decry the violence. Yet while we all say that we hate it, we continue to surround our children with it in their daily lives. As individuals we condemn it; as members of the larger, anonymous society, we love it. Our larger culture fosters it, uses it for entertainment, and sells products with it. Why? Because it is profitable to do so.

From the manufacturers and distributors of weapons, to the media that use violence to entertain, to makers of video games and other toys, entire industries have grown up around violence. A quote from *Today's Child* magazine describes the daily inundation of the violence industry very well: "Although violence has always been part of human history, no generation has ever been brought up with so much exposure to wanton, vivid, immediate violence divorced from moral as well as physical consequences." It keeps rolling on in spite of the fact that the Children's Defense Fund has documented that guns killed fifty thousand children and teens in the twelve years from 1979 through 1991 (approximately the same number of deaths as those of American battle casualties in the Vietnam War). It keeps rolling on even though the National Education Association estimates that more than one hundred thousand students carry handguns to school every single day. Parents who want to raise violence-free children are overwhelmed by a culture in love with it.

Determinants of Violent Behavior

There is no single explanation for the level of violence infecting every corner of our country. The causes are complex and numerous. Family factors, like the absence of fathers, poverty, and racism all contribute to fostering the culture of violence. But there is no doubt that the reinforcement that violent behavior receives from our larger culture exacerbates it and increases the risk factor for everyone.

It might be helpful to conceptualize the risk factors for violence as being contained within three concentric circles surrounding the child. These three circles represent family, the neighborhood, and our larger society. The first and smallest ring is that of family.

Child psychologist Byron Egeland and his colleagues at the University of Minnesota's well known Institute of Child Development have spent 17 years researching the causes of aggressive behavior. According to Dr. Egeland risk factors for violence start in infancy. (As noted in an earlier chapter, how an infant "attaches" to his or her parent(s) influences tendencies toward aggressive behavior later on in childhood.) The child develops greater trust when there is a great deal of nurturing from the parent early in life. When trust is present, the child is more likely to comply with initial rules learned in the socialization process. A child without trust, on the other hand, sees no value in compliance. Children who have either been neglected and/or abused develop little empathy for others, and Egeland's research shows they are also more likely to have an underdeveloped conscience and sense of right and wrong. In view of this, it is not surprising that a large percentage of juvenile offenders have a family history of abuse and/or neglect.

A boy's relationship with his father is a key factor in getting the family support needed to head off violent behavior. Boys raised with a loving and caring father are at a much lower risk for violent tendencies than boys who have no father living with them, or than those whose fathers model violent behavior themselves. Without a strong tie to a healthy parent, particularly his father, a boy's role models become those of our larger society, that are tough and macho. This raises the risk factor for violent behavior.

The healthier the family, therefore, the less likely a child is to be violent later on in life. Attitudes toward violence in the family obviously have an impact; children who see other family members resort to violence in conflict situations carry that experience with them and are likely to adopt it as a model for their own behavior. Of course, even healthy and supportive parents are becoming concerned about violent or aggressive behavior they see in their children. That is because violent behavior is also influenced by the factors of the neighborhood and our larger society.

The next circle that surrounds that of the family represents the child's immediate community or neighborhood. Neighborhoods with high crime rates and high rates of violent behavior pose a higher risk that children who live there will engage in violent behavior themselves. In these environments, children see violent behavior modeled on a frequent basis.

As any child gets older, peer pressure becomes increasingly influential. The values of the peer group are very important and will influence a child to resort to violence when violence is the norm. In addition, when guns are readily available, youths who are more impulsive and less stable emotionally will use them. The statistics bear this out: according to one study conducted by the National Education Association, seventy-five percent of adolescent homicides involve guns. In another study conducted by Northwestern National Life Insurance Company, fifty-nine percent of sixth through ninth graders said they could get a handgun.

The last and biggest concentric ring is that of our larger culture. In addition to those of family and neighborhood, the values of society also influence a child. We are quickly learning how influential these messages are, and therefore need to become more aware of how they are being reinforced in our children.

Before we begin to examine those messages more closely, however, two points should be made. First of all, we need to keep in mind that there is a great deal of interaction between these concentric circles of influence. Larger society influences the neighborhood and the family and vice versa. Factors influence one another.

The second point to stress is that risk factors have a compounding and cumulative effect. In other words, a child who comes from a very healthy family and who lives in a community where violence is not condoned has less risk for violent behavior than one who comes from an abusive family and who lives in a crime-ridden neighborhood. The more risk factors, the greater the likelihood of violent behavior. Nevertheless, even the child who is raised in the healthiest of families and neighborhoods is increasingly at risk because of the powerful influence of the larger society, which, as we'll explore, condones and even encourages violent behavior.

The increased violence in found in American culture influences the level of violence found in all families and neighborhoods. Parents who think they can keep their children safe by moving away from the "rough neighborhoods" are quickly discovering that violence is growing everywhere. In fact, the tendency to flee for safety is not only futile, it exacerbates the problem. When we flee rather than deal with the problem, there are fewer people left behind who are willing to confront the issues and work toward solutions. (Also, the sense of community is lost, and there is less value placed on preserving it.) The strategy of retreating and building walls is not working, because the decay is coming from within. The influence of a culture selling violence is flooding families and neighborhoods across the socioeconomic spectrum.

Violence As Entertainment

As noted earlier in this book, profit is the engine driving the entertainment industry. Promoters have to catch our attention to reach us with their ads, and programs have to stimulate us to keep us tuned in. At the same time, it is increasingly difficult to capture and hold the attention of the American public. There is so much stimulation that media messages tend to blur together. So the task for advertisements and programs becomes one of standing out from the crowd. Violence can do that. Violence gets our attention. Therefore, it has become a favorite gimmick in the repertoire of those vying for the public's attention.

To make matters worse, the public becomes desensitized to the level of violence over time. The excitement generated by one level of violent entertainment gradually subsides with repetition. So to stimulate the same amount of response, the violence must accelerate to another level. And as we become accustomed to that level, it has to go up still another notch.

Professional wrestling provides a clear example of this. Each month, wrestling promoters concoct more outlandish and more violent scenarios to keep fans and viewers involved. Viewers from years ago may recall how wrestlers would throw one another out of the ring, or use ring stools or chairs as weapons. When breaking chairs over opponents' heads lost its novelty, the promoters put the wrestlers in cages ten at a time. The fight is not over until only one "gladiator" (their terminology) is left standing. And although the violence in the ring is contrived, the violence engendered among the fans in attendance is not. Security police patrol the matches and can attest to the high incidence of fights and assaults at such events. (Also, the stereotypes used to appeal to basic ignorant hatreds have escalated. It used to be the American vs. Soviet wrestler was featured. Now there are Middle Eastern, military, and police stereotypes, including at least one brutal "cop" who wields a billy club. In order to increase the "grudge" value and the promise of violence, promoters appeal to racism, sexism, and other of our worst traits and try to inflame them.)

I use professional wrestling as an example because this "sport" is increasingly aimed at children. Wrestling matches are televised on late Saturday mornings right after the cartoons, and at other times that reach an audience largely composed of children. In addition, toys such as children's action figures that depict wrestling stars are big sellers.

The selling of violence as fun is constantly escalating. Many adults have only a partial awareness of how pervasive violence is in the diet of television, movies, music, video games, and toys being fed to America's children. A recent development is the broadcasting of real-life police shows. Instead of simulated violence performed by actors, these new shows have actual footage of real-life crime and assaults, and they are often shown in prime time.

Television Violence

The Center for Media and Public Affairs was asked by *TV Guide* to conduct a content analysis of a typical day of television programming. The staff of the Center analyzed eighteen hours on ten channels on April 2, 1992. (That day, by the way, was quite ordinary. There was no unusual event of civil disorder on the news. There were no atypical movies aired. It was just another day of television programming.)

The ten channels chosen included the three major networks, Fox, public television, and some popular cable channels. In the 180 hours analyzed there were:

1,846 individual acts of violence
175 scenes of violence resulting in fatalities
389 scenes of serious assault
362 scenes of gunplay
673 scenes of punching, slapping. or pushing
226 scenes of threats involving a weapon

Remember, this was a typical day of American television. What's more, other studies confirm these findings. The National Institute of Mental Health, a federal government agency, found that 80.3% of all TV programs contain acts of violence. The typical program includes 5.21 incidents.

What we can extrapolate from these figures is that the average American child will witness approximately two hundred thousand acts of violence on television by the time he/she is eighteen years old. This will include forty thousand murders. The message to our children is that violence is normal—that it is the American way of dealing with problems, expressing anger, settling arguments, and proving oneself.

The media's often-heard counterargument is that television is merely reflecting the violence already present in our society. When we consider the numbers, however, that argument becomes preposterous. As violent as our society is, television is in no way an accurate reflection of it. Research cited by journalist Britt Robson reveals that TV characters are murdered at one thousand times the rate of American citizens.

Clearly, violence is not a necessary ingredient in producing programs that are popular with children. Nonviolent programs like *Mister Rogers' Neighborhood, Beakman's World,* and others have proven to be extremely popular with young viewers.

Movie Violence

Graphic violence in movies has become more extreme as well. The most obvious example can be seen in the popularity among teenagers of the "slasher" film. Unlike horror films of past generations, today's slasher films portray violence at great length and in graphic detail. In the popular *Texas Chainsaw Massacre 2,* for example, people are skinned, burned alive, dismembered, and ground up to be served as chili con carne. All of this is graphically depicted on the screen, leaving nothing to the imagination.

Even though most of these films are rated "R," I have been told by students that they have no difficulty gaining admission to the theaters. Even if they did, it would simply be a matter of months before the films could be rented as videos or seen on cable TV, and would therefore be accessible to any age child. (Video stores generally will not rent X-rated movies to minors, but will rent R-rated videos if the child has a family membership card.)

Most adults have never seen these movies. Many mistakenly assume these teen films are like the horror movies of years past, which may have been scary, but were not a steady stream of blood, guts, and sadistic cruelty.

In spite of the "R" ratings, slasher movies are aimed at the kids' market. Tie-in books and even toys are based on these films and are marketed to children. Several years ago a Freddy Krueger (the facially deformed killer from the *Nightmare on Elm Street* series) doll came out and was only removed from stores after strenuous protests by parent groups. R-rated "Action" movies like the *Rambo* and *Terminator* series are at least as popular with younger audiences as they are with adults. A line of toys accompanies almost all these films, as do promotions at fast food restaurants frequented by children.

Another disturbing development in the slasher and action movie genres is the combination of violence with humor. Perhaps because they are finding it harder and harder to top themselves for sheer gore, it is becoming more common for the hero to make a wisecrack as he machine-guns the bad guy to death. Clint Eastwood's now famous line, "Go ahead—make my day" has become part of modern jargon, and was quoted by none other than the former President of the United States, Ronald Reagan. Such humor further trivializes the violence and gives the impression that killing is fun.

Do these movies affect kids? Consider these examples: In the fall of 1993, teenagers were killed and injured while imitating a scene from the movie *The Program*. In it, a star quarterback proves his toughness by lying down on the white lines in the middle of highway traffic. In a 1992 National Public Radio interview, a gang member told how he was "pumped up" for months after watching *The Terminator.* He described how he and his friends went around looking for fights so they could be just like the hero of the movie.

This type of violence has become so ingrained in our culture that we don't think twice when the star of *The Terminator,* Arnold Schwarzenegger, is held up as a role model for youth. Then-President of the United States George Bush named him as the Chairman of the President's Council on Physical Fitness and Sports. How ironic that we make someone whose reputation is based on the portrayal of violence a national role model for children. We do this at the same time that we wring our hands over escalating violence in our country.

Violence and Music

Music is and always has been a very powerful medium. By combining words, rhythm, and sound, the composer can reflect deep emotions. From love ballads to protest songs, music has been shown to move people. It can move them to sing, to dance, and to act. It can communicate love, concern about injustice, and even mindless rage.

Violence as a theme has increasingly invaded this domain as well. Just as violence can sell movies and TV programs, producers have found that it can sell compact discs and cassette tapes. Once again, it is in the music marketed to kids where this is most true.

We don't have to look far in a music store to find music that degrades women and promotes bigotry. Many lyrics by heavy metal bands are blatantly sexist, racist, and violent. For example, *Girls, Girls, Girls,* a Motley Crüe album, reached number two on the pop charts and sold more than two million copies. It included a song that went, "Those last few nights it [the blade of a knife] turned and sliced you apart / Laid out cold, now we're both alone.../ But killing you helped me keep you home." Kids attending a Ted Nugent concert would hear a song called "Violent Love": "Took her in the room with the mirrors on the walls, / showed her by brand new whip.../ Screamed as she started to slip."

Frequent targets are women, homosexuals, and immigrants. Lyrics off a bestselling album by the group Guns N' Roses included, "Police and niggers—that's right—get outta my way... Immigrants and faggots, they make no sense to me..."

Along with the promotion of violence, it's not uncommon for popular songs to encourage alcohol and drug use. Black Sabbath, for instance, has a song about drinking whiskey and tequila while cruising down the road at 105 miles per hour.

While concerns grow about gang violence, there is a spate of popular songs glorifying membership and the violent behavior that is a part of it. Heavy metal and some rap concerts are often marred by incidents of violence. A Run-DMC concert in Long Beach, California resulted in forty-two injuries. Twenty-five were arrested and twenty-two were treated at Pittsburgh area hospitals after a concert there by the same group.

This is not to say that there isn't good music being produced and marketed to young people. However, there is a growing segment of the music industry that has discovered that violence and bigotry can be profitable. Like in so many other cases, the profits to be made in the music industry become the overriding concern.

Video Games and Other Toys

In 1992 alone, the video game industry in the United States grossed more than $5.3 billion dollars. This is a fast-growing market, and it is overwhelmingly youth-oriented.

Some games are clever, educational and fun. The technology has wonderful potential to teach and entertain. Unfortunately, the easy sell of violence as a theme has taken over. Nintendo, for instance, at one time had cornered eighty percent of the video market, and in 1989 a study by the National Coalition on Television Violence showed that eighty percent of Nintendo games portrayed violence. Another example is the video game that was the country's most popular in 1993—"Mortal Kombat." As I first learned from my young neighbor, the object of the game is not just to kill your opponent, but to master the skills to do it in more and more vicious ways.

Video games are becoming increasingly realistic thanks to advances in graphics technology. Many are produced as tie-ins with popular violent movies. The advertising of these games touts them as both more violent and more lifelike. The ultimate goal is a virtual reality game where the violence is indistinguishable from that of real life.

In video games you get multiple lives, thereby allowing you to "die" over and over again. The winner in these games prevails with greater force and quickness, not intelligence or problem-solving ability. Also, video games are usually played alone and don't encourage cooperation or interaction with other kids. These are all factors to be considered in determining what these games are teaching our children.

Toy manufacturers have often linked their new products to popular movies or television shows. With the predominance of violence as a theme in the media, it's not surprising that other, more conventional toys have followed suit. Today's toys go far beyond the traditional toy soldiers, tanks and guns. New toys like the Rambo 81mm Mortar Thunder-Tube Assault or the Horri-Bull Transformer encourage direct violent play. Even as the safety testing of toys has become more stringent, toy manufacturers have tried to keep up with visual electronic media in their escalation toward more vivid, more cruel, and more graphic violence.

The Effects

Concern about violence as a theme in American culture is not based on a matter of taste; it isn't a matter of some people just not liking it. The fact is that the diet of violence fed to our children is both killing them and undermining the very foundations of our society.

As we've discussed, children learn by imitating the behavior that they see around them. This innate ability to imitate is natural and normal. Particularly when they are young, however, children do not have the ability to distinguish which behaviors should be imitated and which should not. They just imitate the models they have and observe which ones are encouraged or reinforced.

Therefore, the early models that children have are especially influential, because small children don't have any standards for comparison. They don't know what behavior is good or bad—

they just know what is. As a result, a child's family is very influential. First impressions are important for all of us, but first impressions about life come to a child from watching his/her family. It makes sense, then, that children who see violent behavior in their homes are at greater risk for it in their own lives. For instance, studies show that boys who witness abuse directed at their mothers are more likely to grow up to be abusers themselves. Girls who witness this same abuse are more likely to grow up to be abused.

Up to the age of four, a child is unable to distinguish fact from fantasy, even if an adult tries to help the child make the distinction. This explains how very young children become so enamored of fairy tale characters—they are real to a young mind. It explains why young children believe that dinosaurs can talk and fairies can fly when they see such things on television. When we consider their impressionability and drive to imitate, the values communicated to children early in their lives become vitally important. Future learning is compared to these early messages—they form the cognitive categories, or mental "bins" into which future information is stored.

In the previous chapter we discussed how influential television has become in the lives of American children, and how it has become the window through which children look at the world. Television has become their most influential teacher (although other media exert their influence as well). But with the prevalence of media violence, children are learning that violent behavior is the norm. It is exciting. It will make them powerful. It's the way adults resolve disputes. Children imitate the Terminator in the same way earlier generations imitated the Mouseketeers. The process is unchanged. However, instead of wearing Mickey Mouse ears, they imitate karate chops and the use of weapons.

Children will emulate and imitate the models with which they are presented, and models whom they like and whom they find appealing are even more influential. That is why violent heroes are even more harmful than violent villains, according to psychiatrist Dr. Robert Strayhorn.

With violence more and more popular as a theme in entertainment, is it a coincidence that homicide and violent crime rates among youth have steadily climbed as well? The answer from the researchers who have studied the correlation between violent behavior and violent entertainment is clear and unambiguous: the link between the two is indisputable.

The National Institute of Mental Health has documented a broad consensus in scientific literature confirming that children's aggressive behavior increases with exposure to media violence. This consensus was demonstrated across literally scores of studies.

University of Kansas professor Aletha Huston testified before Congress that "virtually all independent scholars agree that there is evidence that TV can cause aggressive behavior."

A twenty-two-year study by psychologist Leonard Eron of the University of Illinois and L. Rowell Huesmann, professor at the Institute for Social Research at the University of Michigan, found a direct correlation in middle-class children between the amount of violent entertainment watched and subsequent aggressive and anti-social behavior.

A University of Pennsylvania study asked a large sample of children, "How often is it all right to hit someone if you are mad?" There was a direct correlation between the amount of television watched and the response to this question, with children who watched more TV answering that violence was acceptable a greater percentage of the time.

Among eighty-five major studies exploring the link between television violence and children's aggressiveness, eighty-four found a positive correlation; the one study that didn't happened to be funded by NBC.

Recent testimony before Congress by the American Psychological Association concluded, "There is absolutely no doubt that the increased level of TV viewing is correlated with increased acceptance of aggressive attitudes and increased aggressive behavior . . . Children's exposure to violence in mass media at young ages can have harmful lifelong effects."

Results of these studies are not well known to the American public, but again, that should not come as a surprise. Why would television and other mass media report to us the unmistakable connection between violent entertainment and problems with violence in society when they have so much invested in violent entertainment?

What Can Be Done?

The epidemic of violence sweeping our society is a concern to all of us. But we keep responding to the effects rather than the causes. During the decade of the 1980s, America doubled the size of its prison population, yet the violence rages on. The increase of expenditures in the criminal justice system is accelerating at a rate four times as fast as our expenditures for education. And while we are concerned as a nation with the rapid escalation of costs related to health care, how many Americans realize that the rate of growth in health care costs is only half that of the criminal justice system? Clearly, we have to find solutions to treat the causes of violence, not just its effects.

It would be naive to assert that America's epidemic of violence is simply the result of too much violence in the media; the roots of violence include racism, poverty, and injustice. However, it would be equally naive to deny that those roots include society's promotion of violence for profit.

Asking media leaders to eliminate violence has proven to be a waste of time. At present, they are only rewarded for producing profit. Violence sells, and media violence will continue as long as it is profitable. The entertainment industry will never regulate itself; in over twenty years of monitoring escalating levels of TV violence there has been no sustained decrease in spite of concerns raised by various public interest groups. When congressional pressure recently began to mount, the major networks agreed to run a "violence warning" for parents before shows that they conclude have unacceptable levels of violence for children. This served to hold off more strict regulations for the networks, but there are two problems with the strategy. First, the networks themselves decide what is acceptable and unacceptable. Secondly, the solution assumes that a parent is present to hear the warning and that the parent will act on it.

The First Amendment Controversy

Since voluntary measures have proven to be ineffective, there is a growing sentiment favoring mandatory regulations that would limit media violence. Whenever this discussion is raised, however, there is an immediate First Amendment frenzy, according to Myriam Miedzian, author of the book *Boys Will Be Boys*. The entertainment industry asserts that any regulations would infringe on First Amendment rights to free speech. Cynics counter that this argument is a smoke screen that is being used to allow the continued exploitation of America's children for profit.

Myriam Miedzian believes that there are solutions that are compatible with First Amendment rights. She asks us to consider that we have a long history of laws and regulations that are meant to protect children. We allow the sale of alcohol, for example, but we prohibit it for children. We allow the printing and sale of pornography to adults, yet we do not consider it a First Amendment infringement when we deny the sale of such material to children. Therefore, laws protecting children from harmful things like alcohol and pornography are not violations of First Amendment rights. When it comes to with radio and television broadcasts, however, the challenge is how to restrict them from children without restricting them from adults as well.

There may be a technical solution. A so-called "parent chip" can be built into television sets so that parents can program the set to receive only transmissions they approve of. Such technology exists today, and could be mass produced. The parent chip could be built into every television. One legitimate concern abut this solution, however, is that it might backfire by freeing up television producers to put more violence on TV. It seems to me, however, that benefits would outweigh the risk.

Such a solution, however, would only work if parents took the responsibility seriously and used it. Unfortunately, many parents have become desensitized as well. They do not realize the impact that media violence has had on them any more than they realize its impact on their children.

The Real Power For Change

Since money drives the machinery spewing out violence, economic pressure may be the best way to stop it. We need to respond in such a way that it becomes unprofitable to exploit America's children. Here are some suggestions:

1. We need to undertake a massive campaign to educate America's parents about what violent entertainment is doing to our children in the same way that this country has educated its citizens about the dangers of cigarette smoking. We need to teach parents in our churches, temples, and mosques. We need to make education on media violence a goal in our PTA meetings. Wherever parents gather, they need to learn that violent entertainment is even more dangerous to their children than not wearing seatbelts. Perhaps federal funds could be earmarked to air TV and other media public service announcements. Just as we have banned advertising of tobacco products on airwaves because they are considered a threat to public health, maybe we should consider the banning of advertisements of violent films and toys.

2. We need to advertise violence ratings of movies, music, video games, and TV shows. Organizations have developed the methodology to rate shows and products, and those ratings should be widely distributed. They could be listed in TV Guide, and they should be in music and video game stores.

3. We should organize boycotts of advertisers of the most offensive shows. As soon as it hits them in the pocketbook, advertisers will begin to support shows that rebuild our society rather than tear it down.

Suggestions such as this one raise legitimate fears in many people. Images of book burnings and McCarthy-esque hunts come to mind. Please remember that I am not advocating destroying video or audio tapes or games or prosecuting their creators. I am suggesting that we wake up and not reward advertisers and manufacturers of harmful material with our patronage. If we tell them with our purchasing decisions what we want for our children, they will get the message. The first step is for us to realize what is happening and how we can influence it.

4. We need to take a careful look at the toys we are buying for our children. Do the toys we buy reflect someone's market plan? Are we always buying the latest merchandise that ties into a new TV show or movie? We need to buy toys for our children that encourage imaginative, fun play, not toys that encourage modeling of the latest violent storylines from TV or movies.

5. We need to take personal responsibility and personal action. We need to prohibit our children from watching inappropriately violent shows. We need to encourage the teaching of nonviolent conflict resolution in schools. And most important, we need to make absolutely certain that we are not modeling violent behavior ourselves.

If a company was selling food to children that was tainted with disease and made them sick, we'd take action in a second. But over time, little by little, parts of our society have been rewarded for poisoning our children with violence. The effects are just as serious, and it is just as vital that we take action.

CHAPTER 7

Self-Discipline and Our Instant Society

Discipline. The word itself is imposing to many of us. It may bring on images of attending to unpleasant or tedious tasks, of forcing ourselves to do things that are devoid of enjoyment. Discipline was not always thought of this way, but this is how it has come to be regarded in our society. Little wonder, then, that it has become so hard for us to instill a sense of self-discipline in our children.

As parents we are faced early on with the following question: How do we effectively impose discipline on our children? Walk into any bookstore and you are presented with an array of books describing discipline techniques. Parenting classes also abound that are meant to help us clarify and implement new ideas.

We are fighting an uphill battle even as we search for more effective strategies. We discuss techniques, but we know that self-discipline is what our children really need. And self-discipline is not highly valued or reinforced in our society. In fact, the booming messages in our culture advocate self-indulgence, the antithesis of self-discipline.

Self-indulgence can promote profits in a consumerist economy, since the more self indulgent we are, the more we will spend on ourselves, and the more accouterments of leisure and affluence we will pursue. Self-discipline may be healthy for an individual person, but it is not a value in a system promoting acquisitions and excess.

All of us are born with a wide variety of drives and needs. Those drives and needs are essential for our survival as human beings. Our need for food and water, for example, motivates us to eat and drink, ensuring our physical survival. However, these needs and drives often conflict with one another. A child's drive for curiosity may at times conflict with a need for caution—a caution that keeps the child from serious danger. A teenager may have a high need for peer acceptance, but this need for acceptance must be balanced with the need for safety if the peer group pursues a dangerous activity.

Our needs and drives are like a group of horses. Unbridled and untamed, they can pull us apart. If they can be harnessed, however, they can act as a team and can transport us to new heights. The process of taming our drives is what self-discipline is all about. Without self-discipline, we are at the mercy of our drives; with self-discipline, we can accomplish great things.

This ability to regulate ourselves is needed every day of our lives. The child in seventh grade who wants to complete a book report has to be able to keep her body in the chair and her mind focused long enough to complete the task. But there may be a variety of drives competing with her desire to complete her assignment. She may be struggling with the impulse to watch TV, to make a peanut butter sandwich, or to tease her brother. All of these drives are competing simultaneously. She will only get the book report done if she has the self-discipline to control the impulses until she's finished.

Self-discipline is necessary for successful living in all areas of activity. It is essential in managing our emotions. Anger, for example, is an emotion aroused in us when we feel we are being treated unfairly. It's an emotion that is very helpful and useful—without it we could be habitually mistreated or taken advantage of. It helps us survive, but it is important for us to be able to be in charge of this emotion lest it get out of control. Without self-discipline, I might lash out in anger at someone for being fifteen minutes late before discovering I was actually fifteen minutes early.

Our ability to manage our drives distinguishes us as human beings. The higher functions of the brain are able to regulate and manage the lower functions—our judgment can manage our drives.

This ability to discipline ourselves is not only necessary for an individual to function well, but is also essential for the survival of a democratic society. Our country is comprised of millions of individuals and groups. If each individual or group blindly pursued its own needs or gave vent to its own drives, the result would be chaos. For our society to survive, we must be able to balance conflicting needs. Everyone cannot always have exactly what they want. This system involves compromise and cooperation, and without self-discipline, those two things are impossible to sustain.

However, while self-discipline is indispensable for an individual person and for a society to function well, it is not something that happens automatically. Like many other skills, it must be developed over time. It is built by practice, repetition, and reinforcement, and its development has to be valued as a goal. But that's where the catch comes: while self-discipline is vital for healthy development, it is not something that is valued in our larger society. It is not modeled and it is not reinforced. In fact, the value of self-discipline is undermined by society's messages.

Two crucial ingredients that contribute to self-discipline are the ability to delay gratification and the ability to seek and achieve balance. As we shall see, American culture of the late twentieth century sees little value in either of these. The opposite of the ability to delay gratification is the need for instant gratification, and the opposite of balance is excess; these opposites are two major values of our popular culture. The remainder of this chapter deals with our instant society and its value of instant gratification. Chapter Eight explores our culture of excess.

Our Instant Society

There is an obsession in American culture with anything fast. Products are constantly promoted on the basis that they are "ready in seconds." "Do it now" is the message; we are told that it is foolish to wait for something if we don't have to. If you want to go on a vacation, just go. Don't worry about paying for it until next month's credit card statement arrives.

Everything we do is in a rush. We have express tellers at the bank, express lanes at the supermarket, instant potatoes, speedy lubes for our automobiles, books on one-minute management, and one-week diets to lose twenty pounds. A heartburn remedy that brings relief in thirty seconds is always in danger of losing out to a remedy that works in twenty seconds.

Our fixation on speed is probably related to the belief that "we can have it all." In our attempts to "have it all," speed is important because it enables us to pack in as much as possible so we can race on to the next thing.

If something takes too long, we as a society are not interested. And if fast is good, faster is better. Particularly in the last twenty years, we have become obsessed with finding ways to do things faster. From microwave ovens to food processors to computers, products are all designed to gain speed and save time. Theoretically, those saved hours and minutes should give us more time for relationships, families, and leisure. But in spite of all the time saving, we have less time than ever before.

The fast pace of our lives is also evident in the rushed development of our children. We encourage them to read earlier, learn their numbers earlier, and grow up earlier, in spite of growing evidence that our efforts do not improve their academic performance or social skills.

New things are presented to children at a very fast pace. For instance, the speed with which images flash on the screen during Sesame Street is very hard for a human teacher to compete with, and the popularity of video games is also related to speed and pace. Things happen very fast in these games, with the participant rapidly moving through video mazes to rescue captured allies, find treasure, and, most often, to blast video adversaries. To the aural accompaniment of explosions, fisticuffs, buzzing electronic music, and other sound effects, a player experiences multiple "lives" of mayhem. The games are often ingeniously complex, with lots of hidden shortcuts. The pace is fast, faster, and fastest. Time penalties create a sense of urgency, and results of actions are quick. A push of the control button annihilates an enemy in a fraction of a second.

When you consider how our society values speed, the design of video games makes perfect sense. We like things to happen fast, and we don't like to wait. We also like things to be resolved or "fixed" quickly, and want our efforts rewarded without delay. In other words, we have become a society obsessed with instant gratification. A recent television advertisement plays upon this need:

The ad presents a beautiful, successful-looking young couple on vacation. They are dining at an outdoor table at a luxurious tropical resort. As they wind up their stay in paradise, the woman looks wistfully at her partner and says in a half-sigh, "It went by too fast, didn't it? I wish it weren't ending." Her male partner responds, "It doesn't have to." The next thing we know, a phone call is made, all plans and responsibilities are put on hold, and the beautiful couple extends their stay in paradise. All this in less than thirty seconds—thanks to their determination for instant gratification of pleasure, and their credit card.

The credit card company that is responsible for this ad is the one with the slogan, "Membership has its privileges." It proudly touts the fact that there is no cap on the amount of credit available to those with a good record. The whole scenario is presented as a near-fantasy for adult viewers. Most of us wish we could do something so capricious, but see it as possible only in our daydreams. The ad's message that a phone call can arrange everything—including a stay in paradise—is the opposite of the kind of work ethic that built this country. It flies in the face of the philosophy of working hard to achieve a goal, of being patient, and of the need to save up to earn something worthwhile.

With instant gratification messages being promoted on a regular basis, is it any wonder that American people in general have a declining rate of savings per capita, and that the average American saves a much smaller portion of his or her weekly salary than workers in comparable industrialized nations?

The direct message of this type of advertising is that we should all be able to have what we want when we want it. Waiting for something is portrayed as an infringement on our right to have it now.

Children, by their nature, are impetuous and impatient. They are already inclined to want their needs filled immediately. When this natural impatience is reinforced in a thousand different ways by our culture, the drive toward instant gratification becomes overpowering.

If children are taught that they don't need to wait, it's very difficult for them to develop life skills that are so important for maturity. Many important things in life take time and patience to achieve. Mastering complex concepts in school, for example, require persistence and time. Significant goals such as learning to play a musical instrument often require dedication over a period of many years, sometimes with little in the way of tangible rewards along the journey.

Children can be conditioned to expect instant reward either directly or indirectly. The direct message comes from the media, that tells kids they should have what they want right now. Most of us have heard words like the following ones thousands of times: "Don't delay. Act now so we can ship it to you overnight." Children are also taught instant gratification indirectly in the modeling they see in their parents and in other adults. When we respond to messages such as: "Have your credit card number ready. Our operators are waiting for your call," the meaning of our actions is not lost on our children. Many catalog order companies are open twenty-four hours a day, so whenever the impulse to buy strikes, we can get service with absolutely no delay. And when we behave in a way that implies that waiting is to be avoided at all costs, our children are watching then, too.

Unfortunately, we are not only taught to get what we want quickly; we are also taught that difficult problems should be solved quickly. Many television shows, for example, present very difficult personal problems for their characters, only to have them resolved in thirty minutes or less—(twenty-two minutes not counting commercials). So not only do we have two-minute popcorn, we also have thirty-minute resolutions of complicated human dilemmas. Since everything about our lives is supposed to be fast, problems, we are told, should be resolved quickly. There is no time to deal with complicated and sensitive interpersonal issues, so we look for a facile strategy—or worse, a medication—to put them behind us immediately.

Elementary school teachers can attest to the impatience of today's children. Often, if a problem cannot be figured out quickly, the youngster wants to give up, and may consider himself to be slow or stupid. After all, in our society, competence is equated with lightning-fast problem-solving.

The fast pace of our lives, coupled with the racing images on television and video games, create a constant state of stimulation and excitement for children. By comparison, working through complicated math problems or reading a book can seem boring.

Still, no matter how we try to avoid them, there are times when we are not engaged with stimulation. The fact of the matter is that learning to cope with boredom is a part of life. But the implicit message of our culture is that boredom is bad and must be avoided at all costs. Couple this with the fact that doing "boring" things can make a child a social outcast, and we can see the pressure children are under to maintain a constant state of stimulation. Some children do it with nonstop activities; many others turn to TV or video games. Anything that cannot measure up in terms of immediate sensory stimulation or excitement is condemned as uninteresting by kids, and the messages sent by our society are responsible.

Once again, teachers are hard-pressed to compete with electronic media. If a school lesson is not entertaining enough to fully occupy their attention, students will entertain themselves or create their own excitement, often by acting out.

No Pain, No Gain

The needs for constant excitement and instant gratification are often accompanied by an intolerance for pain and discomfort. Our culture abhors pain; we have a quick remedy for every type imaginable. As a consequence, our children are taught that pain, be it physical or psychological, is always bad and should be avoided at all costs.

I am certainly not arguing in favor of pain. However, temporary discomfort and distress is part of everyone's life. Therefore, it is essential that we help our children learn to cope with pain, particularly the pains of boredom, disappointment, and rejection. Coping with pain means developing qualities like perseverance, patience, and the ability to delay reward.

These skills are not learned automatically; they are taught. And the lessons are not always easy or pleasant. I remember a scene from my childhood that was repeated many times over. During the summer, the ice cream truck would make its rounds. As it came down the block, kids scattered in all directions to get money for a treat. I was no exception, but nine times out of ten, my mother would say, "I'm sorry, but not today." As I got older, I learned to argue more forcefully. On many occasions, I accused my mother of being too tight with her money. "Can't you afford a dime?" I pleaded. I can still recall her response: "It's not the money. I just want you to learn that you can't always have what you want when you want it." I didn't understand that lesson at the time, but it made more and more sense to me as I got older. In a small but important way, my mother's response helped prepare me to deal with frustration and disappointment.

Of course, saying "no" to an insistent child is a lot more difficult than saying "yes." A parent's aversion to the pain of saying "no" often leads to giving in rather than holding the line. And it is understandable; temper tantrums in a store or a freeze-out sulk by an adolescent can be painful. It can seem much easier to say "yes," as it makes the present moment quieter and more peaceful. But what is accomplished? What is taught?

The trouble with always following the path of least resistance is twofold. First of all, the child does not learn the difficult but important lesson about the need to delay gratification. Secondly, saying "yes" too often can create a pattern to which there is no end.

To avoid a case of the "gimmies" when shopping, children can be prepared ahead of time as to what they can expect to get (if anything). Understandings can be worked out where a toy or treat will be purchased only as a reward for cooperating or helping, or after a certain amount of allowance or birthday money is saved. If parents are consistent with these requirements, their firm responses can provide a wonderful opportunity for children to learn about responsibility as well as the need to delay gratification.

It may seem ironic that the primary reason parents give in to children is that they, too, want to avoid pain. Actually, it is a good example of the following point: our everyday actions as adult role models can teach our children a great deal, in either a positive or negative way. If our children see us overusing our credit cards or shopping constantly without real need, can we realistically expect them to heed our pleas to be patient and to do without the treat they want? The behavior we model is vitally important, because our children will hear this message almost exclusively from us. Teachers or other adults may communicate it at times, but our culture advocates just the opposite of patience and restraint. Children hear and see an infinite variety of very persuasive messages to do it or get it now. The odds are stacked against us, but if parents can be fair, firm, and set good examples, there is a good chance that children will learn this important lesson. At the same time, we can work to change the misleading messages of our culture.

Another product of our culture's value of instant gratification is our tendency to be a "throwaway society." When something doesn't work to our satisfaction, we get rid of it. Many household items are designed to be discarded after usage. Disposable lighters, disposable diapers, and disposable food containers are a few examples. The message is clear: it's easier and faster to throw something away than it is to fill it, clean it, or fix it.

This "throwaway" mentality has created some serious environmental problems. Our discarded material has fouled the earth, water, and the air. Furthermore, we are quickly running out of disposal sites for all the things we throw away. The rise of recycling in recent years is a positive sign that we can slow down the throwaway machine if we put our minds to it.

This throwaway mentality is very attractive to kids, who, as we've noted, tend to be impatient. Learning patience is a natural part of their maturing process, although the lesson doesn't take hold if it is not taught and reinforced. Therefore, it is not surprising that kids who are still learning or who have yet to learn patience are often ready to discard something immediately when it doesn't work.

Our obsession with speed, the avoidance of pain, and the throwaway mentality can all combine to create some very real problems for children as they grow older, particularly if those tendencies in our society are not tempered with a parent's lessons of patience, perseverance, and commitment. Take their potential effects on our children's relationships, for example. Any long-term relationship will have its share of ups and downs, joys and pains. If a child has learned not to tolerate pain, to discard things if broken, and to constantly look for new and exciting things to occupy his or her attention, then the child will find it hard to honor a commitment through the difficult times as well as the good.

The effects of our instant society also apply to one of our nation's most insidious problems: drug and alcohol abuse and dependency. Drugs and alcohol are the ultimate quick fix. They relieve pain and provide an instant reward. One of the most addictive properties of crack cocaine is that it produces its euphoric effect in a matter of seconds. When we keep in mind how tempting it is for us to look for fast solutions and how our society encourages that behavior, it is easy to see the huge profit potential in mood-altering substances.

Of course, the drug and alcohol problem is multifaceted. It would be overly simplistic to say that it is entirely a result of our society's attachment to quick fixes for pain. On the other hand, however, it would be naive to deny the connection. It is not surprising that a society that values very fast results, seeks to avoid pain, and prizes instant gratification has an enormous problem with drugs and alcohol. Those who say that we will never get the problem under control until we address our society's love affair with the quick fix are probably correct.

Another effect of America's obsession with speed and instant gratification is the involvement of children in adult activities at earlier and earlier ages. Rather than childhood being a time of slow ripening, it is increasingly seen as a stage to be gotten through as quickly as possible. This pressure is evident in many ways: Children are pushed to read earlier. Their peer role models in the media often appear to be grown up well beyond their years. Little Leaguers are provided with full baseball uniforms, just like adults. In these and a number of other ways, adults encourage kids to act grown up, and we reward them with attention and praise when they do.

In past generations, it was a comic image in a family photo album: a little girl or boy dressed up in mom or dad's clothes, swimming in oversized garments, playing a game of "let's pretend." The kids in our photos today are just as likely to be dressed in adult clothes; the difference is that their dress consists of well-tailored versions of adult fashions. Today's kid may be dressed in ninety dollar designer jeans, eighty dollar shirts, and one hundred and fifty dollar athletic shoes, all featuring the same labels as their parents' clothes.

It is easy to imagine how profitable it is to "hook" kids on expensive clothes with designer labels. For many merchandisers it's a matter of taking advantage of whatever the market will bear. If the extravagant designer market can be extended to kids, then it means more profits falling to the bottom line.

Today's children are encouraged to be like adults in more ways than just fashion. Sexuality is another example. In spite of widespread concern about the growing number of teenage pregnancies and the increase in sexual activity among young boys and girls, many of society's messages actually encourage children to be sexually active. In many television sitcoms, for example, young children say precocious adult things to get laughs. More and more of these remarks have a sexual subtext. Even though they are played for "cute," they send a message to kids that this behavior is entertaining.

Maybe the most blatant exploitation of kids is the attention we lavish on "supermodels" who are often in their late teens or very early twenties. They are presented as the ideal of feminine beauty and are portrayed as seductive and sophisticated. These young women are exploited in the selling of everything from automobiles to shaving cream.

It was a few short years ago that Brooke Shields, a young teenager at the time, first appeared in magazine ads with clearly sexual overtones. She quickly became almost infamous for print and television ads in which she appeared wearing skin-tight designer jeans, declaring, "Nothing comes between me and my Calvin Kleins . . . nothing!"

The message to young girls was clear: they could be glamorous and desirable by being as seductive as possible. Of course, what the jeans maker wanted was more sales, and a deliberately controversial ad campaign was the vehicle chosen for getting them. The advertising industry has never been accused of being troubled by matters of conscience; since those jeans ads first appeared in the mid-1980s we have seen a plethora of similar ad campaigns for various products featuring ever-younger-looking seductive models (primarily female) promoting a variety of products.

It is ironic when we consider the furor caused in many communities by controversy around school-based sex education classes. Some parents become absolutely livid when the possibility is raised that their children will be taught about sexuality as part of a health curriculum. Yet there is seldom any similar storm of protest about the sex education our children are getting from exploitive advertising and television programs.

Old Beyond Their Years

Many five-year-olds "can't wait" to go to school for the first time. Seven-year-olds "can't wait" to be eight-year-olds. Fifteen-year-olds "can't wait" to get a driver's license. "Can't wait" is a natural part of childhood, whether it's for a vacation, a privilege, a toy, or a step along the path of maturity. The natural impatience of youth can make waiting seem endless and unbearable, and our society's message that waiting is unnecessary and not to be tolerated greatly exacerbates these feelings.

Waiting, however, has two very important benefits for children. First of all, it teaches patience and the ability to delay gratification. Secondly, children have the pleasure of something to look forward to and the satisfaction of reaching an awaited event. Having something to look forward to can provide motivation and excitement in anyone, adult or child. Half the fun of a vacation for instance, is in the planning and anticipation. As the countdown progresses, the energy builds. This is true of short-term goals as well as long-term. In fact, part of the excitement of childhood itself is looking forward to the opportunities or privileges coming at a later age. Anticipation gives meaning to passages. Even as small a thing as being able to stay up fifteen minutes later can be a thrill to a child who has just reached her seventh birthday.

The other side of the coin is this: if a child has been allowed to do everything at a young age, then she has less to look forward to. The child has, to a certain extent, already done or experienced it all. There are no goals to strive for, and the child's life can become directionless.

There is a very real danger that this is happening to today's children. Kids who do everything at a young age can get bored all the more easily because they have nothing to look forward to. The rites of passage into adulthood are devalued, and this can lead to a loss of respect in children for both adults and themselves. And the force responsible for this threat boils down to greed.

More and more adult things are being pitched at kids. As we saw in Chapter Four, advertisers realize that today's kids are not the fifty-cents-a-week allowance crowd of years ago. The burgeoning children's market is targeted by advertisers of big-ticket adult items like expensive clothes, high-tech sound systems, and electronic gadgetry. There are entire stores specializing in formal wear and high-priced designer labels for children.

With the pressure to have adult things at an earlier age comes pressure to do adult things at an earlier age. It is not uncommon, for instance, for private dance or music schools to rent an area's finest concert halls to hold music and dance recitals for students as young as four years old. When top dollar is paid for formal clothes, instruments, and accessories, nothing less is acceptable. So whether they are taking lessons for fun or as the beginning of a serious pursuit, children are learning and performing in settings that are as thoroughly professional, high-tech, and state-of-the-art as those used by top level professionals.

Should any of these young performers succeed in making a career in the arts, what would they have to look forward to? They have already performed on the finest stages. This kind of acceleration can short-circuit the process of gradually building up to special experiences and accomplishments.

Children's athletic programs offer another example. Young children are often organized into highly-structured teams with high-quality uniforms. Many take numerous out of town trips, staying overnight in hotels and eating in restaurants. For the very elite players, these trips may be to other states, or even to foreign countries.

If a child has been going on road trips for years, what can be special about high school sports? I've heard high school athletic coaches complain that incoming players lack motivation because they feel that the teams don't do anything exciting. A trip fifty miles away is not going to make a big impression on a youngster who has already taken many team trips out of state.

A similar pattern can be found in children's entertainment events. Concerts—especially rock concerts—are being targeted to younger and younger children. Parents are barraged with requests from eight- or nine-year-olds to get tickets to the latest event, and these tickets may cost the equivalent of several months' allowance. The concerts themselves are well orchestrated, with levels of sensory stimulation that approach or exceed overload. Entertainers go to greater and greater lengths to outdo one another. After viewing some of these concerts, local events operating on modest budgets pale by comparison. A child may look with scorn on going to a play put on by a community theatre, or attending a free concert in a local park.

Social relationship standards are subject to the same pressure on children to be sophisticated and act grown-up. Kids are dating at younger and younger ages. I've had teachers give examples of boys and girls in elementary school already "going steady."

The present generation of kids is obviously not the first to complain of boredom. The word "boring" has been a staple of kids' vocabularies since time immemorial. However, the low threshold of boredom among many of today's youth is a concern. It's hard for them to get excited about everyday life when they've had such a highly stimulating diet.

A second issue is perhaps even more serious. As humans, we become accustomed to certain levels of stimulation. Once that happens, we need stronger levels of stimulation to become excited. This is true both physiologically and psychologically.

In the chemical dependency field, this phenomenon is called "tolerance." As a person gets accustomed to the effects of alcohol or drugs, he needs larger and more frequent doses to get the same effect. As tolerance increases, the use escalates until it finally gets out of control.

As kids are exposed to more and more stimulating experiences at earlier ages, they develop a tolerance. To feel excitement, they need experiences that will bring them to a higher level. How will kids get pleasure out of a school band concert if they're used to multi-million dollar professional events? How will kids be satisfied with holding hands in junior high school if they've already been dating for four years?

Many of our kids who have had the freedom and opportunity to do many things at a younger age have become jaded. They are bored with day-to-day things. Their senses have been overloaded, and it takes more and more for them to get their interest. For them, it becomes a matter of finding something to do after they feel like they've done it all.

It does not seem unreasonable to hypothesize that this is another factor in the serious drug and alcohol problem among our youth. Drugs and alcohol are attractive because they alter moods. They give the user an immediate "kick." If a youngster is bored with so much of life, it can be very tempting to turn to—or depend upon—drugs or alcohol for that new kick.

It can be very tempting for us to want our kids to have and to do the best. However, we may unwittingly be creating an appetite for stimulation that renders normal life dull. In addition, we are robbing our children of the excitement of looking forward to special events and of achieving milestones by themselves.

When children are allowed privileges and exposed to different and exciting experiences on a gradual basis, they not only have things to look forward to; they also avoid the problem of accelerated tolerance and sensory overload. This principle applies to all areas of a child's life, and while it does not rule out special treats or events, it is important to consistently maintain it. By definition, if something is repeated often enough, it is no longer special.

We can always loosen up restrictions. However, once children accustom themselves to a steady diet of high stimulation, it is very difficult to reverse the trend. We need to be mindful of this as we determine which activities are appropriate for different ages. Childhood should be a period of discovery and excitement, not of jaded cynicism and rewards without effort.

America's children desperately need to be taught the skills of self- discipline; they need to learn how to accept delayed gratification. Their own development and our society's future demand it. But it's hard for America's adults to teach them that because we, too have been inundated by the same cultural imperative to "have it now" and "do it now."

We must combat the messages of the instant society, and to do so we have to first learn that we can't always have what we want exactly when we want it, whether it is relief from a headache or the new car we really can't afford. Then we have to teach our children. We have to teach them that part of living involves pain, and that part of growing up is learning how to deal with pain rather than running away from it. We need to remember the words of poet Eve Merriam: "No wonder grown-ups don't grow anymore. It takes a lot of slow to grow."

CHAPTER 8

"Winning Isn't Everything—It's the Only Thing"

Nearly all parents want what is best for their children, and hope they will lead successful lives. The problem is that our society's definition of "success" is "coming in first." That message is all around us—we see it in advertising slogans such as "Go for the gold," "We're number one," and "Faster, Tougher, Smarter."

When it comes to selling products and services for kids, the fears of parents for their children are irresistible targets for advertisers. If our child isn't outperforming other children academically, athletically, or socially, we may worry that he or she will not be able to compete later on in life. Advertising fans the flames in an effort to persuade us to purchase goods and services that will give our kids an edge, or at least keep them from falling behind the pack.

Encouraging high goals and achievements in our children is obviously not bad. Competition and pressure to excel, in appropriate doses, can even be effective motivational tools, and one can persuasively argue that learning to deal with a certain amount of stress from competition is part of growth. It can be a necessary and positive aspect of the maturation process.

Competition then, is not inherently unhealthy. The problem occurs when competition gets out of balance in a child's life.

Several years ago there was a book on the bestseller lists entitled *In Pursuit of Excellence*. The sequel appeared several years later, and was titled *A Passion For Excellence*. This progression from "pursuit" to "passion" is telling; it signals that even something like excellence can get out of balance when it changes from a desire to an emotional need.

After I spoke at a conference on parenting several years ago, a parent from the audience approached me and told me about a teacher who would always return test papers in order of the students' scores. Her daughter often received her paper near the end—her scores were among the lowest in the class despite hours of studying. She was not failing the tests—she was getting Cs— but she was in a class of high achieving students. She would come home from school in tears, screaming that she was stupid and that she wanted to drop out of the class. She had told her mother how ashamed and embarrassed she felt when she was among the last to get her test back. "Every kid in the class knows how dumb I am, " she cried. When this parent went to talk to the teacher, she was told that this procedure was a "good motivational tool."

At another conference, a parent told me about a high school social studies teacher who announced to his students at the beginning of the term that in his class there were only two grades: A and F. It could be that this teacher was trying to convey a message that anyone is capable of "A" work. Certainly he used this grading method as an attempt to motivate students. However, the message that many of the students took from this was that if your work wasn't excellent, then it was worthless—a failure.

If we reflect for a minute about how important it is for children to feel competent and successful in order to develop self-esteem, then we start to get a glimpse of the harmful effects of an overdose of a "passion for excellence." Excellence is a relative term for each child. Excellence for a child with limited abilities in mathematics might mean he gets seventy percent of the answers right, even if he ranks twenty-eighth out of twenty-eight on a test. If the only measure of excellence is being number one, then it is impossible for more than one student to feel proud of her achievement or confident about her abilities.

Many teachers like those described above are trying to challenge the complacency of kids in our instant society who seem very content with mediocrity even though they are capable of much more. I am certainly not advocating the abandonment of standards, and agree with educators who are identifying the need for greater self-discipline. Although I concur with their goals, however, the methods chosen often unwittingly reinforce the societal message that coming in first is the ultimate objective.

As mentioned in the previous chapter, balance is a fundamental ingredient of self-discipline. But while balance is essential to developing self-discipline and crucial to rear healthy children, it is not a value of the society we live in. Excess is the value reinforced today, not balance. Today's children are pushed to be and have the most and best of everything. Society's message is that if you aren't the best, then there's something wrong with you. If this message seems hard to accept when spelled out so blatantly, consider the following example of this kind of thinking in action:

In January of 1994, the Buffalo Bills made their fourth consecutive trip to the Super Bowl. They had lost each of their three previous Super Bowl games. In the days approaching the game, media commentators around the country were talking about what a shame and disgrace it would be if the Bills lost again for the fourth year in a row. As game day approached, the possibility of a fourth consecutive loss was discussed almost as much as the game itself.

The Bills did lose the game, and in the days and weeks that followed, articles were written about the entire Buffalo community sinking into a depression. Media personalities around the country made the Bills the butt of jokes and hoped out loud that the Bills would never get to the Super Bowl again, thereby saving themselves from future disgrace.

But put the team's performance in perspective. How many teams have ever been to the Super Bowl four times? Not many. There were twenty-six teams sitting at home that day wishing they could trade places with the Bills. Of all of the football teams in the NFL in 1994, the Buffalo Bills had out-performed all but one. Yet after the defeat an entire community felt deflated, let down, and embarrassed. Why? Because being number two is not good enough in America.

The fixation with being number one is not reserved only for our highly paid professional teams. College and even high school coaches report being under increasing pressure to win. Those whose teams don't measure up to community expectations are more and more frequently in jeopardy of being fired; their ability to teach sportsmanship and other values does not enter into their job evaluation.

In a Twin cities suburb recently, a group of parents was successful in having the high school girls' volleyball coach removed. She was not a poor coach by any standard; her teams had enjoyed their share of success. She was dismissed because she lacked national volleyball connections, which limited her ability to get national recognition for her players.

Shortly thereafter, a sports columnist writing for the Minneapolis *Star-Tribune* described how "mad dog parents are on the rampage in most every suburb." These parents constantly and loudly complain about coaches who they feel aren't good enough. This columnist pointed out that in a six-year period, one affluent school district fired more coaches than all the athletic departments of the collegiate Big Ten conference combined.

Many educators I've spoken with are distressed at the pressure put on kids to win in competitive sports. Student athletes will often risk their health to gain an advantage. High school athletes have told me in interviews that there is widespread use of steroids in athletics, even though their use violates the rules and poses a serious health threat.

A high school hockey coach with a successful program once told me how parents had pressured administrators to have him removed because he hadn't taken the team to the state tournament. There are constant problems with coaches recruiting all-star teams among nine- and ten-year-olds in spite of explicit rules prohibiting such activity. Coaches can accomplish this by hand-picking the best athletes and refusing to take others, or by filling the roster up with recruits before other players ever find out about the registration process.

Sports medicine specialists report another indication of the overemphasis on winning and being the best. There has always been concern about injuries incurred in youth athletics, but in the past decade a new concern has emerged: injuries from overtraining. Physicians now list damage by overtraining as one of the most serious health threats to young athletes. Such injuries were almost nonexistent among children just fifteen years ago, according to the experts.

Sprained ankles from basketball games or the bumps and bruises acquired in football are the sports injuries many of us think of first. However, the injuries among young athletes participating in solo, non-contact sports is rapidly increasing. For instance, almost twenty percent of kids in gymnastics clubs suffer injuries. "The injury rate is unbelievable among pre-pubertal girls who constantly train," said Dr. Sheldon Burns, a physician who specializes in sports injuries and works with professional sports teams. Female gymnasts are four times more likely than other athletes to suffer lumbar spine injuries, he reports, and they also have a relatively high incidence of eating disorders.

It has been estimated that more than a third of competitive youth runners will develop leg injuries from overtraining. Damage to shoulders and to rotator cuffs from too much practice are the biggest problems for swimmers. Tendinitis and similar inflammations are a growing threat for young tennis and baseball players. And although pediatricians are raising concerns about these issues, "playing hurt" is seen as a badge of courage in a society fixated on winning.

A decade ago, the governing boards of most states' high school athletic leagues had strict rules curtailing off-season competition. Now, most have succumbed to the pressure from non-educators, and the rules have disappeared. Anything goes when it comes to camps, off-season leagues, and junior programs. Many youth sports have become strictly organized, with teams of grade school kids playing seventy- to eighty-game seasons. With the addition of practice time, some kids are involved with their organized team every day of the week. There has been a dramatic shift in youth sports away from a sense of enjoyment, physical fitness, and sportsmanship to intense competition, winning at all costs, and being number one.

There is also pressure for kids to begin intensive training and specializing in a sport at earlier and earlier ages. Professional tennis stars who break into the limelight during their teen years have often embarked on their career soon after they started walking. Expensive summer camps run by big name professionals are flourishing and luring younger and younger children. This intense specialization is often fueled by the promise of big money. Bob Trenary, father of Olympic figure skater Jill Trenary, described in a radio interview how many families will mortgage themselves deep into debt in order to have their children positioned for a spot on a national team. The attack on skater Nancy Kerrigan just prior to the 1994 Winter Olympics revealed to what lengths some will go in chasing the gold medals and the millions of dollars that go with them.

As "coming in first" has become emphasized, some parents have become overinvolved in their kids' athletic achievements. One high school basketball coach explained it this way: "Their social fabric becomes their son's or daughter's involvement in athletics. They get to know the other parents. They meet for breakfast on the way to the game. Then one of their kids starts to fall behind his peers athletically, and the parents become embarrassed. They can't handle it." The result is more pressure on the child and more pressure on the coaches. The coaches are told that they're not being fair, or that they are not properly utilizing the talents of a particular youngster.

Earlier in this book I referred to kids who are spending inordinate amounts of time sitting in front of a television set. Now I'm talking about kids with a fixation on being number one. Although these types of youngsters are very different, both have something in common. Both are responding to society's pressure toward excess and imbalance.

When winning is the dominant value, moral and ethical values inevitably suffer. Several years ago, the following tragic story was reported in a St. Paul, Minnesota suburb:

A youth hockey team had traveled out of town for an important game. During their overnight stay at a hotel, several stars on the team raped an eighth grade girl who had accompanied the team as a cheerleader. When she reported the crime, she became the object of ridicule and persecution. She was criticized for pressing charges, and many adults tried to blame her for the crimes committed against her. The reason that the community failed to support her was that she had accused the stars of the team, and the team could not win without them. She was also accused of hurting their careers. The young girl continued to be harassed for blowing the whistle on the hockey stars until she committed suicide three years later.

After her death, her parents talked about the torment she had endured during her high school years for "ruining" the team. The rapists had become untouchable because they were "winners," and winning meant everything. That girl and her family were the victims of our society's obsession with winning and stardom as much as they were the victims of a group of morally bankrupt people in their community.

With winning being so important, honesty is increasingly lost as a value. Cheating to win has become so common that most Americans are no longer surprised when a scandal is uncovered at one of our colleges or universities. Youth sports organizers report they must be ever more watchful lest parents falsify birth certificates. Some parents do this so their kids can compete at a higher level at a younger age; others do it so their children can excel against younger competition.

Winning As The Predominant Value In Life

Our society's preoccupation with winning is not restricted to the athletic field. Programs that promise to "teach your preschool child how to read" are heavily marketed to parents. These programs make money because parents are led to believe that learning to read early will give their child a leg up on the competition. However, in his book, *The Hurried Child,* psychologist David Elkind explains that such programs not only fail to give children an advantage, but may negatively affect a child's reading skills later on. This adverse reaction is probably caused by the pressure kids feel at so early an age. In addition, young children who are pushed to read at an early age usually accomplish this by "sight reading."

They often don't learn the phonetic skills necessary to help them decipher the more complex words they encounter as they get older.

Another example of the obsession to be number one is the competition to get into the "right" schools; among certain circles it is more intense than ever before. There are preschools in the United States that allow parents to put their children's name on their waiting lists as soon as the pregnancy is confirmed. Some schools have thousands of applicants for 100 slots or less. And before their children reach preschool, these parents buy books by the thousands with such titles as *Teach Your Baby To Read*, *Teach Your Baby Math*, and *How To Multiply Your Baby's Intelligence*. Children will often respond to this pressure to excel by either over-achieving (with high anxiety) or by "burning out" and losing interest later on.

The ways in which summer camps have changed offer another example of the societal message to be number one. While there are still many camps that offer a variety of enjoyable activities and experiences, there has been a dramatic increase in the number of "specialty" camps.

The recreational camp experience most adults remember was usually spent near a lake, and the campers would learn how to swim, play games, and do crafts. They met new friends, sang camp songs, and teased the counselors. These kids might leave these camps with a slight sunburn and maybe a touch of poison ivy, but with a ton of happy memories. Contrast that experience with today's camps for children that offer accelerated and intensive courses in stock market timing techniques, computer programming, or intense athletic training.

The marketing slogans and advertising copy for some of these camps tell us a great deal about their philosophy. One ad boasts of "high-powered hockey training." Another informs parents that "tennis instruction for fifteen hours a day is available." Even when these camps are not harmful to children in themselves, they reflect the obsession our society has with being number one and gaining the upper hand over the competition.

Benjamin Franklin wrote the following motto in *Poor Richard's Almanac:* "If something is worth doing, it is worth doing poorly." What this means is that there is value in trying things out, and in doing things at which we do not excel. We do not have to be tennis pros in order to benefit from the exercise of playing. We don't have to produce masterpieces in order to make our efforts at painting or sculpture worthwhile.

Even if we fail to achieve a goal, the attempt is worthwhile; learning from failure can often be more valuable than learning from success. And learning how to cope with failure is an important step in the maturation process. Life is full of its ups and downs. Learning how to cope with them is essential.

With these factors in mind, we can better understand how our societal preoccupation with winning can have a number of negative results. The child with limited skills in a particular activity gets the message that he/she is somehow an inferior or incompetent person rather than someone whose talents lay in different areas. There is no value attached to being a well-rounded individual.

For the child who does win a lot, the situation is just as bad. A great deal of pressure is created to keep coming in first, and an activity that was once a source of enjoyment can become a hated chore. Also, those youngsters who pick up on how society values winning can develop a distorted view of their own worth and importance with respect to other children.

A Call For Balance

Success and excellence are obviously not bad things. But we can motivate our children to do their best without giving them the message that winning is everything. We need to balance achievement with respect and consideration for those who have not been given as much raw talent, but who want to participate in an activity nevertheless. The attitude of being committed to doing something for the learning and enjoyment derived from it is to be admired.

If all the hours of practice, study, and honing of skills have not been tempered with the everyday lessons that tell a child you can't win all the time, then there is a strong possibility that the depths of disappointment can swallow that young person up. No one can be the best in every situation. There can be much pride and satisfaction in participating in an activity without being the best. When a passion for excellence means never being satisfied with our best effort, then excellence becomes a tyrant.

It is possible to be competitive without having to be number one. Indeed, encouraging that balance between being motivated to compete and knowing oneself well enough to be satisfied with one's best efforts can make a person a more effective competitor. The balance of competitive spirit, high self-regard, and respect for others is the combination for a healthy personality. Our society does not glamorize this combination, but we need to help our kids develop this balance.

There are a number of specific ways we can do this. First of all, we should encourage our children to try out many different activities as they grow up. They don't need to specialize at a young age without ever having different experiences. Secondly, we should take our cues from our children with regard to readiness. There's a big difference, for example, between a child asking questions that signal a curiosity about reading and a parent who enrolls his or her child in the latest program to teach preschool children how to read just so they'll have a leg up on the competition.

Parents should involve themselves with the leaders of children's activities and tone down a coach's enthusiasm, for example, when it seems to be getting out of kilter. Children involved in sports should have reasonable and balanced practice and game schedules that allow time for other activities.

Another important suggestion is to talk about a healthy balance and to model that ourselves. Sometimes parents get so wrapped up in their kids' activities that they have more invested in them than the kids do themselves.

CHAPTER 9

"Whoever Gets The Most Toys Wins"

The war is on. The struggle is for the hearts and minds of America's kids. On one side is a set of values and traditions that could be summarized by the words of the fox in Saint Exupery's novel, *The Little Prince:* "It is only with the heart that one can see rightly. What is essential is invisible to the eye."

On the other side is a consumerist machine that bombards our kids daily with this message: "Whoever gets the most toys wins." What is seen as essential in this way of thinking is not only very visible, but preferably has a conspicuous price tag on it.

Some of us are still shocked when young teens murder one another for a jacket with the "in" label. Teachers see their students' work suffer because of long hours spent during the school week working to earn extra money—money that is by and large spent on recreation, fast food, stylish clothing, and "toys." Parents worn down by their children's constant pleading break down and buy them what they so desperately want, only to find that it isn't enough. There is always something new to be had.

We shouldn't be shocked or surprised at any of these phenomena. America's kids are only doing what we've taught them to do. Our culture's overwhelming message is that happiness is found in material possessions, so, being good learners, America's children see accumulating things as the pathway to happiness. They're doing so with a single-mindedness that is, not coincidentally, rewarded and reinforced by society. They must not only get what they want—they must get it now.

Parents at my seminars frequently report that their kids are increasingly reluctant to do jobs around the house unless they're paid. "The notion of family responsibility seems to be slipping away," they complain. But this should not be surprising, either. Our kids are taught that money and what it will buy are the most important things in life. As we've seen, the voice of consumerism is blasted to our children at every opportunity, even while we maintain that our own values are quite different.

Our attitudes about money and materialism provide the clearest examples of the dichotomy between our private values and the values that our larger society promotes and teaches our children. In a 1990 Gallup survey, seventy percent of Americans polled said that there is too much emphasis on trying to be rich in the United States. By contrast, almost seventy-five percent of college freshmen that same year reported that it was "essential" or "very important" to be well off financially. More significant than that figure, however, is its rate of change over the years. That same question has been asked of college freshmen for many years by UCLA's Higher Education Research Institute. In the past two decades, the percentage of students who stressed the importance of being well off increased by more than sixty-seven percent.

Reporters for *The Washington Post* interviewed high school students about their attitudes toward money for an article about the expectations of kids. "I want to be rich—I do!" said one student. "I know myself, " added another. "I'm money-hungry." The reporters found startlingly inflated expectations about money across a spectrum of socioeconomic classes. One girl confided that she expected to make her first million dollars before she was thirty-five. The authors concluded, "In the schoolyards, hallways, and lunchrooms . . . the talk concerns material success: how best to get it, and what most can deter it."

As seen in the Gallup survey, many Americans worry about our society's preoccupation with money and materialism. Many are concerned with the effects of these obsessions on our children. But these worries are by and large confined to private reflections and small group discussions with other parents. The voices of our larger society do not echo these worries. In the anonymous American society of the late twentieth century, consumerism is proceeding full speed ahead. "Shop 'till you drop" is the operative expression, and our kids are picking up the message loud and clear.

A primary goal of producers of consumer goods and services is to create desires. This is not to say that there is no money to be made in making products that fill needs in society—of course there is. But continued growth, expansion, and ever-increasing profits are to be found in constantly adding to our list of desires. If a manufacturer or service company can create a new desire, then before long we may come to think of it as a need. As we try to fill more and more "needs," the market keeps expanding.

Our society has gotten so good at creating desires that we Americans are pursuing them even beyond our ability to pay. The credit card explosion provides an important insight on this phenomenon. According to HSN Consultants, in 1980 there were 526,000,000 consumer credit cards in circulation in the United States. That's more than two cards for every woman, man, and child in the country. Ten years later, that number had almost doubled, to just over one billion cards.

But while the number of credit cards doubled, the number of people holding the cards did not. Cardholders increased in this ten-year span by only twenty-nine percent, which means that people were carrying more cards. The truly amazing statistic, however, concerns credit card debt. From 1980 to 1990, credit card debt more than tripled—from eighty billion dollars to over a quarter of a trillion dollars! Clearly, we Americans are buying things way beyond our means to pay for them. But no matter—the worry we hear about in the media is not that we're overspending. The worry is that we will cut back. The goal is to constantly increase "consumer spending" to help the economy.

Credit cards reflect the twin American values of materialism and instant gratification. With a credit card we can not only get what we want, we can get it right away, even if we can't afford it. It should come as no surprise that credit card companies are now offering cards to kids. Their parents, of course, must sign the application and are financially responsible for the charges incurred, but it's the child's card. After all, it's never too early to get kids hooked on buying on credit.

The Twin Voices: Programming and Advertising

In earlier chapters we discussed the power and influence of two of contemporary society's voices: television programming and advertising. We explored how they work in tandem as very powerful influences in shaping popular values. Furthermore, we discussed how those voices are almost exclusively enlisted in the effort to sell things. It's not surprising, therefore, that money and material possessions are dominant values in our larger society. They are the values promoted by these twin voices.

Television programming and media advertising teach two very prominent messages. The first message is that personal happiness is of paramount importance. The second is that happiness is found in having things. These messages are taught in the programs we see and in the pitches we hear. Sometimes they are taught directly and explicitly. At other times they are taught indirectly and subtly.

We've touched upon the fact, for instance, that the socioeconomic status of most television characters is significantly above that of most viewers. The cars they drive, the houses they live in, the clothes they wear are all very nice and very expensive. And this is not confined to fictional characters; whether it be the hero of a sitcom or the local news anchor, most of the people we see on television look, dress, and have things that reflect financial success.

Today, kids are well aware of the financial motivations and the financial status of their sports heroes. The best athletes are constantly in the news because of their demands for more money, or because they are leaving one team for another to get a bigger contract. These same sports heroes drive the fanciest cars, wear the most expensive clothes, and generally model the life of the wealthy. Of course kids want to be like them. Kids have always emulated top athletes.

As we've discussed, advertisers often try to link products with feelings of happiness. On a subconscious level, the audience is meant to associate happiness with the article or service being sold. Since the people seen in advertising are usually placed in settings that connote wealth and material success, it is easy to imagine how children can easily develop the idea that becoming rich is extremely important to their future happiness.

In Chapter Four we touched on the fact that the messages about money and materialism that are promoted through television programming and advertising are more and more aimed at children. A further indication of this is the doubling of the number of children's magazines in the past ten years. The number of children certainly hasn't doubled in that time, so how do we explain the one hundred percent increase in magazines marketed to children? The answer is simple: magazines are financially supported by advertisers, and as we've seen, advertisers have a newfound inter-

est in children because of the money they control and the purchases they influence.

Only one in three American households has children living in
it, yet those are the ones that spend the most money. Households
with children are the most lucrative consumer segment in the
United States. As a result, they are a primary target of those with
goods or services to sell.

The influence of children within that market segment has grown
very rapidly during the past twenty years, for three reasons: First
of all, at the start of that time span, parents were having fewer
children, and so a greater portion of the family's financial resources
were focused on each child. Secondly, there are more children living in one-parent families. While these families may not have the
financial resources of two-parent families, their children tend to
do more of their own shopping, as well as more buying for the
rest of the family. Thirdly, almost seventy percent of households
with children are dual-career households. Research shows that
children with two working parents are more involved in shopping
decisions; like single-parent children, they are involved directly
by doing more buying themselves, and by their influence on their
parents' purchasing decisions.

The figures show that the influence of children on consumer
purchases is out of balance demographically. In 1980, children
under twelve represented 17.8% of the American population. In
1990, the percentage was 17.6%. Although the size of the group
remained more or less constant as a percentage of the population,
their economic influence climbed, according to Texas A & M
Professor James McNeal. Because their influence extends far
beyond what their numbers would suggest, children are targeted for
more and more consumer messages.

In some specific categories, in fact, children are the dominant
shapers of the market. Although they are by no means the only

customers of fast food restaurants, ninety-four percent of six- to fourteen-year-olds visit one monthly, and twenty-two percent visit more than twice a week. This fact is not lost on fast food companies or the advertisers they employ. Professor McNeal's research shows that eighty percent of frozen snack purchase decisions are influenced by children, and sixty percent of canned pasta decisions are made by them. The list goes on and on, and while these facts may surprise most of us, they are well known to marketing professionals. Advertisers and manufacturers are fighting to establish brand identification and loyalty among four-year-olds because they know how profitable it can be to influence the desires of children.

Those targeting children also have increasingly powerful data at their disposal. Reports like *The Kids Study,* published by Simmons Market Research Bureau, promise the reader that he or she will have access to comprehensive research data on children ages six to fourteen. The report provides manufacturers and advertisers with demographic data, media habits, purchasing power statistics, brand preferences, and even the Sunday comic strip preferences of America's children. All of this helps the marketers make sure their aim is on target and that their pitches create maximum results.

Even tobacco advertisements appear to be aimed at the young. Is it happenstance that this coincides with the rate of new adult cigarette smokers finally starting to decline in the United States? Not surprisingly, the only segment of the population with an increasing rate of new smokers is youth. The "Joe Camel" advertising campaign launched by RJR Nabisco which features a cartoon character clearly targets the young. RJR Nabisco, of course, denies it, in spite of the fact that children can identify Joe Camel at a rate higher than they can identify Mickey Mouse.

The success that tobacco marketers are having with kids is all the more amazing when we consider that it is illegal for kids to buy cigarettes. Unfortunately, the legal barriers pose little obstacle for kids who want to smoke. Not only can they buy them from vending machines, but even some merchants often ignore the laws. Smoke Free 2000, an organization dedicated to the reduction of tobaco usage, reports that kids have little difficulty buying cigarettes wherever and whenever they want.

The evidence we've seen all points to the fact that children are being singled out as targets of consumer advertising. It is not surprising that they are getting the message; the values promoted by our materialistic society are taught very widely and very well. Children have more money and consumer goods at their disposal than ever before in large part because they have been taught to demand more. More than forty percent of eight-year-olds have their own televisions, for example, which in turn increases their exposure to messages telling them to want more.

The impact of this pressure to buy, buy, buy can be serious on children. Preoccupation with money and consumerism can distract them from other, more age-appropriate concerns. It can create an insatiable appetite for possessions that overrides other values, affecting both their expectations and goals.

Children who negotiate with their parents about getting paid to clean the bathroom, for example, are reflecting the material orientation of our larger society. Just as their sports hero holds out for the best deal, they may feel they can bargain in a similar fashion. There is no value to be seen in helping out; anything with real value, they have learned, has a price tag attached to it.

The polls cited earlier show how the expressed goals of college students have shifted away from helping others and toward career paths that will maximize income. Many higher educators are concerned that the best and brightest American students are bypassing careers in such areas as education and science to enroll in business or professional programs. When asked about their motivation to pursue their course of study, the students' responses are more and more frequently oriented toward income.

The practice of making choices about work solely on the basis of monetary reward is not restricted to college students. Every year the percentage of high school students who work at jobs during the school term keeps rising. It now exceeds fifty percent. Ellen Greenberger, a Professor in the Program in Social Ecology at the University of California at Irvine, and Lawrence Steinberg, a professor at the University of Wisconsin in Child and Family Studies, wrote an important book about this topic entitled *When Teenagers Work*. One of its conclusions is that "A job is no longer a rite of passage to adult responsibility, but a way of celebrating the materialism of a selfish society."

Children working at wage-earning jobs are not a new phenomenon. For centuries children have worked on the family farm or in the family business. In earlier generations, youth would serve apprenticeships. They would not only pick up the craft or skill from their adult mentor, they would also come to value the work ethic and the sense of responsibility that came with it. Work was truly a rite of passage. (To be fair, there were, and still are in some countries, sweatshops that exploit children as workers. Child labor laws were enacted in the United States because we saw the ill effects of this exploitation; we acknowledged that it is wrong to take advantage of children in this way.)

Yet today's jobs for youth too often offer little educational value. Millions of teens work in dead end, unchallenging jobs in a workplace dominated by uncommitted part-time employees. This situation is at least partly caused by companies wanting to avoid the expense of providing benefits and who want to pay little more than the minimum legal wage. Kids, of course, cannot command better treatment or opportunities because of their lack of training and experience.

In the first half of this century, most working teens contributed to the family and/or saved their money. Today, studies show that most teens do not contribute to the family, but rather spend most of their income on entertainment and other personal expenditures. Teens who do save their money often do so to purchase a car. High school administrators can attest to the need for ever-expanding high school parking lots as more students demand this expensive status symbol.

Considering the growing appetite among teens for consumer goods, a particular finding of Greenberger and Steinberg's research becomes quite alarming. They reported a direct correlation between the net value of items a teenager purchases with his/her own money and the risk for destructive behavior.

What Can Parents Do?

The following are some concrete suggestions for parents:

1. Before we can complain about excessive consumerism or competition among our children, we must first look at ourselves. It could very well be that they are learning about excess partly from us. If we buy on impulse, overextend our credit, shop for recreation, or are always pursuing the latest model car or gadget, it will be very hard to talk credibly to our children about wanting too much. By the same token, if we become consumed by work and if we are always relentlessly pursuing the next income level, then it will be very hard for us to talk to our children about striking a balance in their lives.

2. Today's children cannot be shielded from all messages of consumerism. However, keeping consumer impulses within bounds is important. We should discuss advertising with our children and help them understand how it works. We can explain how desires are created and how they are converted to needs by sophisticated manipulation. We can teach our children that material possessions can provide us with satisfaction, but that long-lasting happiness is found in other places.

3. We need to spend twice as much time with our kids and half as much money on them. The majority of today's kids don't need more money. Almost all of them need more of our time, more of our guidance, more of us. It's easy for us to get some temporary peace and quiet by buying our kids off, but all we do is create a greater appetite for things. That appetite is already whetted by the messages that our culture communicates to our kids.

It is usually easier for parents with disposable income to spend money than it is to reprioritize time commitments. It is also easier to spend than it is to wrestle through difficult issues that involve a certain amount of conflict. Taming the spending monster is not easy to do; retailers and advertisers don't want us to do it. But it is something we must do for the sake of our kids.

4. It is not the responsibility of children to set boundaries and limits for themselves. That's the job of adults. There are many voices kids hear that tell them to consume, buy more, do it earlier, enjoy it all now. Because of kids' natural impatience, they are more than ready to heed those voices. If anyone is going to set the limits so that balance can be maintained, it has to be the adults in a child's life.

I'm not speaking here of a knee-jerk "no" to everything. Rather, I mean the ability to negotiate meaningfully with our children while we realize that at some point we have a responsibility to draw the line.

5. Children need to learn the importance and value of money. They also need to learn about the responsibility that comes with having money. If they always get what they want without budgeting, saving, and waiting, they are deprived of those important lessons.

When children express a strong desire for something that costs money, it is important that on at least some of the occasions they must make an investment in it. Perhaps they could save up for a percentage of the cost. Or, to counteract the "buy now, pay later" mentality, parents can adopt the "lay-by" approach. That was a purchasing method that was popular a number of years ago, whereby an item could be set aside with a downpayment, but wouldn't actually be acquired until it was paid for in full.

At times kids will respond to a parent's refusal to purchase something with "I'll buy it with my own money," or "I'll get a job to pay for it." Letting kids purchase things with their own money may be appropriate at times, but parents should be prepared to extend the refusal even if the child's own money is going to be spent. Depending on the item in question, the response may need to be, "I'm sorry, but you can't get that, even with your own money." As for allowing their teenagers to get jobs in order to finance purchases, parents need to exercise their authority in making sure those jobs do not interfere with other priorities. This will be dealt with further in Chapter Ten.

Naturally, each adult may act on these suggestions in slightly different ways. Whatever the specific approach, however, parents need to plan and implement a strategy to counteract the "gotta have it now" frenzy promoted by marketers.

CHAPTER 10

"What's in It For Me?"

The ancient Greeks called a person who did not care about others an "idiot." Such a person was considered to be trapped in a fixation on his or her own individual needs and wants. He was also thought to be a liability to the community, because he did not contribute to the general welfare.

The Greeks also handed down the myth of Narcissus, the youth who fell in love with his own reflection. Because of his self-absorption, he was turned into a flower. To this day, a "narcissist" is someone who is selfish and egocentric.

As these examples illustrate, the ability to help others and to put the needs of others ahead of our own has long been considered both a personal virtue and an important ingredient for the larger community. Shakespeare wrote: "It is one of the most beautiful compensations of this life that no man can sincerely help another without helping himself." John Kennedy exhorted us all to strive for selflessness in his now famous words: "Ask not what your country can do for you. Rather ask what you can do for your country."

Our civic and religious traditions honor those who make sacrifices for others, those who put the welfare of others ahead of their own: Sister Kenny, Martin Luther King, Mother Theresa, Dorothy

Day, and Cesar Chavez are just a few examples. We honor these people and hold them up as models because they were able to transcend their own wants and desires in order to help others. People's lives were improved and communities were enriched through their efforts.

Within our families, generosity is a quality we try to teach our children, partly because it is so important in our ability to get along. In the book *The Education of Little Tree* by Forrest Carter, the character Little Tree remembers, "Grandma said when you come upon something good, the first thing to do is share it with whoever you can find. That way, the good spreads out where there is no telling where it will go." Lessons such as these are taught by parents and teachers to children through stories, examples, and songs. However, this theme, like many others in our society, is being overwhelmed by messages that exhort us to "pull our own strings" and to "look out for number one." In our society there is an enormous emphasis on self, a preoccupation with "me." Our children still hear encouragement to be generous and to help others, but they increasingly hear messages telling them to consider one question and one question only: "What's in it for me?"

To be sure, children need to learn an important balance between considering their own needs and those of others. The tension between self and the community is a healthy one, and should never disappear. Children should learn how to identify their own needs and desires and they should feel that it's okay to get those needs and desires met. Children should also develop enough self-respect to realize that they have a right to express their opinion and to ask for what they want.

At the same time, however, children should learn that others have rights, desires, and needs as well. At times those rights, desires, and needs will conflict with their own. However, a healthy person can strike a balance and at times can forego her own satisfaction for the sake of someone else.

Helping children learn the value of both attention to personal needs and generosity is essential. Without an appreciation of themselves, children would be unable to set their own goals and work toward achieving them. They would be unable to stand up for themselves, to express their own opinions and convictions. Without an appropriate measure of "selfishness," children would constantly repress their own legitimate desires and needs.

On the other hand, if children weren't taught cooperation and generosity, they would run roughshod over others' rights. Their aggressiveness would limit their ability to resolve conflicts and negotiate compromises. If everybody is "out for themselves," a sense of community quickly erodes. The rule of the day becomes "might makes right." And if cooperation, generosity, and the value of giving aren't learned, then we will live in a world where everyone is concerned only about themselves. Unfortunately, while our society has plenty to say about the value of selfishness, it is not nearly as interested in promoting cooperation and generosity.

During a concert, singer Peter Yarrow of the group Peter, Paul, and Mary recently commented on the shift in values away from generosity and toward self-absorption by his observation of the evolving titles of popular magazines. First, he noted, we had *Life*. From there we went to *People*. More recent popular magazines are entitled *Self* and *Me*.

In Chapter Five we discussed the influence of television as a teaching tool. A content analysis of television shows was reported on by Cornell University Professor John Condry in his article, "Thief of Time, Unfaithful Servant: Television and the American Child." His findings revealed that sixty percent of television's value messages promote the importance of personal and individual happiness. His study found that in popular American culture, children are taught these lessons about the road to happiness:

- •Wealth is the key to the good life.
- •We should get what we want when we want it.
- •Happiness is found in things.
- •Satisfaction only comes from a constant diet of excitement.
- •Personal enjoyment is of paramount importance.

If we recall that the primary function of television is to sell merchandise, it is not surprising that the models of happiness we see depicted are upbeat, beautiful people immersed in the pursuit of their personal ambitions and surrounded by material goods. This is the image that sells. But while the media is selling products (including its own programming), it is simultaneously teaching and reinforcing the value of selfishness. Other values are being crowded out while fewer and fewer messages in our popular culture are teaching children the values of generosity and sacrifice to counterbalance the emphasis on self-gratification. Our children are not learning about balance—they are learning the values of the marketplace: get what you want and get it now.

The Self-Help Industry

Self-absorption is not only promoted through electronic media. It is increasingly promoted in print, and through my own profession, psychology. The past fifteen years have seen the rapid growth of a relatively new genre of books and periodicals, and the growth of a new industry—the self-help industry.

Although self-help books have been around for a long time, they were once a relatively minor part of the publishing business. Twenty years ago there were no bookstore sections called "Self-Help." Today, that section can be among the largest in the store. Indeed, there are entire stores that specialize in these books.

Let me be clear: there is absolutely nothing inherently wrong with self-help and personal growth. Many books in the self-help category are excellent, and contain valuable information. The point I am making is once again about balance. Valuing self needs to be balanced with valuing others. Respecting the self needs must be balanced with respecting others. Pursuing selfish goals needs to be tempered by a concern for the goals of others. Some of the current self-help literature fails to maintain that balance.

The enormous popularity of the "codependency" movement is a good case in point. This term was originally coined in the late seventies to describe the effects of alcoholism and drug addiction on people in close relationships with the alcoholic or addict. It was a very helpful concept that helped teach people that their well-intentioned behavior could actually "enable" a loved one's addiction, allowing it to continue. (Shielding an alcoholic or addict from the consequences of his actions is a prime example of "enabling" behavior.) The term raised the awareness of millions of spouses, children, and friends of chemically dependent persons and encouraged them to get help for themselves.

However, while it started off as a helpful concept, the term "codependency" quickly became overused. Its definition became broader and broader, until it was used to cover almost all behavior. One national expert on codependency made the claim in the early eighties that ninety-six percent of the population was codependent in some way. Assertions like these led to a humorous analysis done in 1987, which found that if you calculated the rates proposed by the codependency professionals, you ended up with more codependents in the United States than there were people!

The effects of this "national curse" were likewise exaggerated. An extremely popular author in the codependency field seriously compared codependency with medieval plagues, and actually stated that they didn't "even compare to the ravages of our compulsions caused by codependency." The jargon of codependency became infected with hyperbole and generalizations, until any act undertaken on behalf of another person could be criticized by affixing this popular label to it.

My main critique of the codependency movement, however, is not about the exaggeration done by its proponents. It is based on the effects of the codependency rhetoric on our notions about helping and sacrificing. In many circles, altruism and unselfishness became symptoms of a disease. One definition of codependency by a popular author was "a disease of people whose problem is an excessive tendency to help other people."

In the original use of the term "codependency," family members learned that sometimes their best intentions to help the alcoholic were not helpful at all. Their behavior often protected the alcoholic from the effects of her drinking and prevented the alcoholic from realizing how destructive the addiction really was. In this context, therefore, such attempts at helping were not benefitting anyone.

The negative impact of the codependency movement came when the original meaning of the term became blurred by overuse. Within years it had been broadened to describe the entire human condition. The criticism of trying to protect and help loved ones, while valid in the example above, was broadened as well. Soon millions of Americans were being called "codependent" or "dysfunctional" for having an "excessive tendency to help other people." What had been admired as a virtue for thousands of years had suddenly been diagnosed as a disease more serious than the Plague. Sacrifice and altruism were unhealthy impulses to be held in check; detachment and the maintenance of personal boundaries became the new ideal.

This misuse of the codependency concept creates two serious problems. First of all, the overuse of the term does a real disservice to people who are truly caught up in the destructiveness of an abusive relationship, or who live in a chemically dependent family. The word has been spread so thin that it has begun to have no meaning at all, and does not impart the seriousness of such a situation. Secondly, and more to the point of this chapter, the codependency movement has resulted in the generalization that all helping behavior is "dysfunctional," another term that has also become so broad that it can only be defined as "bad." The codependency movement began as an important effort to help people climb out of the pain caused by addiction. Ironically and tragically, it ended up undermining the very value of helping in all too many circumstances. It began to reinforce other cultural messages that promote selfishness.

The troubling evolution of the codependency movement reflects the growing notion that education and self-improvement is worthless if it doesn't help us directly, either by making us love ourselves more or by helping us put money in our pockets. People pack into auditoriums by the thousands to hear motivational speakers across the country. Their seminars promise to deliver the secrets of fulfillment, success, and happiness. The business sections of most Sunday newspapers carry announcements about such sessions on a regular basis. The common theme in all of them is that happiness is related to personal success and the accumulation of wealth; education for its own sake is never the point. In fact, the personal wealth of the speaker is often offered as proof of his or her legitimacy.

These modern-day revivals are yet another indication of the value we place on material things. There aren't many high-profile seminars these days on topics like "How To Help Millions," "Unleashing the Secrets of Altruism," or "Unlimited Generosity." And if wealth and the selfish pursuit of personal comfort are our ultimate goals as a society, how can we expect our children not to adopt them as their own?

The Effects of the "What's In It For Me?" Mentality

Author Robert Bellah, a Professor of Sociology at the University of California, Berkeley, and his colleagues conclude in their book *Habits of the Heart* that late twentieth century Americans' preoccupation with personal ambition and consumerism is a major contributor to the fracturing of our society. In a newspaper interview he described these factors as a cancer eating away at our national heart. Our overemphasis on the self, he said, is "rendering much of the country's middle class incapable of a commitment to their most basic institutions: marriage, family, religion, and politics." He went on to warn that "this individualism may be threatening the survival of freedom itself."

The effects of our societal reinforcement of selfishness as a value can be seen in examples like the following:

1. The growing gap between rich and poor. The prevailing political attitude of the 1980s was that individuals had a right to do their own thing unencumbered by government. Laws were changed to encourage the wealthiest among us to increase their assets. Theoretically, their success would "trickle down" to the rest of the people, thereby benefitting all.

The results of this officially sanctioned selfishness are getting clearer all the time. At this point in our country's history, the gap between the "haves" and the "have nots" has never been wider. Not only did the affluence not trickle down, it further polarized the rich and poor.

2. The scarcity of favors. The Search Institute, an organization dedicated to research about youth, recently surveyed ten thousand teenagers. In the survey, the youngsters were asked whether they had done something helpful for someone else within the previous month for which they had not been paid. Thirty-three percent of the teens reported that they had not done a favor for free for anyone in the previous month. A full seventy-five percent reported that they had spent less than two hours out of a potential 720 helping someone without being paid.

Charity organizations throughout the country report the difficulty of attracting volunteers. It seems that spending one's discretionary time making or spending money is crowding out time spent in service to others. Barbara Dafoe Whitehead reported a telltale statistic in her article in the April, 1993 issue of *The Atlantic*. She cited research that shows that less than fifty percent of all adult Americans today consider sacrifice for others to be a virtue.

3. The self-interest of politics. A major issue in the U.S. Presidential campaign of 1992 was that the government was being controlled by special interest groups. William Greider wrote an important book on that subject entitled *Who Will Tell The People?* In it he described how our political system has become unduly influenced by special interest groups pursuing their own selfish agendas without regard for the common good.

4. Our difficulty in making commitments. With the question of "What's in it for me?" being so prominent, Americans have an increasingly difficult time making commitments. Whether the commitment is to a marriage, to an employer or employee, or to our children, as soon as times get tough the prevailing social message is to cut our losses and get out. There isn't a great deal of societal support for seeing things through in the face of pain or discomfort. We are encouraged to do whatever it takes to make us feel better now.

5. The popularity of the idea that sacrifice is stupid. As noted earlier, one effect of the "what's in it for me?" attitude is that virtues like sacrifice and altruism come to be viewed as foolish. Although these two virtues are the bedrock of a healthy community, they are made to seem senseless in a culture that overvalues personal glory and personal accumulation of money and goods.

What Can Be Done?

Our children are being raised in a culture that does not adequately support the values of generosity, cooperation, and sacrifice, yet these values are essential if our society is to flourish. It is therefore incumbent on all of us to teach and reinforce those values. We can encourage them in the following ways:

1. Model altruistic behavior. Do our children see us helping out others without being asked? Do they see us going out of our way to do a special favor for someone? The behavior we model is very important. We need to show them the benefits of volunteering time and sharing resources with others. The example we set will be far more powerful than any sermons we can give them.

2. Assign chores and responsibilities. It is important for kids to understand that a household functions best when everyone chips in to help out. Although it may be appropriate at times to pay kids for special jobs, it is also important that they do some chores just because they're part of the family. This applies on a community level too, whether it means helping out at the recycling center or shoveling snow from an elderly neighbor's walk.

3. Contribute earnings. As kids get older and begin to earn money, it is important that they learn to save a part of it for the purpose of contributing it to others. Whether funds are donated to your church, to a local foodshelf, or to a national or international charity, the act of giving is more important than the amount.

4. Community service. Our typical responses to our kids' complaints of boredom are to suggest ways for them to play or to be entertained. At least part of the time there should be encouragement to spend time doing something for someone else. Author and youth researcher Kurt Hakop has a helpful bit of advice on how to encourage kids to get involved in helping others: "You can preach at them. That is a hook without a worm. You can order them to volunteer. That is dishonest. You can call on them: 'You are needed.' That approach will hardly ever fail."

CHAPTER 11

Reclaiming America's Children

The effects of our society's messages are clear. The underlying problem—the exploitation of our children for profit—is also clear. Our children are buying into a set of values that we as a society have taught them. Although they conflict with our personal values, we should not be surprised that they are adopting them. Children have always learned the values communicated by the world around them.

Each of us as parents must identify the values we have intentionally taught and displayed to our children. But as we've seen, we must also ask ourselves another question: What values have we as a society taught our children?

While the following is by no means a complete list, it identifies the marketplace messages being conveyed to our children that were covered in the preceding chapters of this book:

1. Happiness is found in having things.
2. Get all you can for yourself.
3. Get it all as quickly as you can.
4. Win at all costs.
5. Violence is entertaining.
6. Always seek pleasure and avoid boredom.

This is what our society is teaching our children. Every morning when we pick up our newspapers we see more and more of the consequences of this "education." We don't need to go over the alarming statistics again. We know that our kids are in deep trouble because of what we as a society have done.

The Search For Scapegoats

As the situation worsens, we should be searching our collective soul for real answers and solutions; instead, we often look for scapegoats to blame, and for quick fixes. One of the most frequently cited scapegoats is the American school system.

Recently I was being interviewed on a national radio show about the plight of our youth. After several minutes of discussion, the host paused, and with great dramatic effect asked me, "Don't you think, Dr. Walsh, that all of these problems are the fault of the schools?" I was dumbfounded when he boiled down the fault for all of the troubling circumstances surrounding our children to one culprit. But looking back, I understand why he did it. In the face of an overwhelming problem, this radio host, like the rest of us, wanted someone to blame. I tried to explain why I disagreed with his assessment, but he would hear none of it. He had it figured out to his satisfaction: the schools were to blame.

Our schools are not the culprits. Schools are dealing with the results of America selling out its children. This is not to say there aren't problems in our schools or that there aren't things we need to change. But to blame our schools for the attitudes and values our children are adopting is akin to blaming physicians for their patients' illnesses. For the most part, schools try to instill positive values in our children. It is when society's values influence their effectiveness (as in the case of Channel One) that their messages become mixed.

The fact is that children are going to school already wounded by a society that undermines positive values. Teachers can't teach as effectively because their hands are full dealing with students' social and emotional problems tjat hinder learning. I've talked to many talented teachers, some of whom work twelve hours a day. Nearly all of them are discouraged. The needs of the children they try to teach are so overwhelming, and our society doesn't seem to support them. Instead of holding up teachers as role models, we look to entertainers and athletes.

Our schools are affected by the same values of our contemporary culture as we are as individuals. They certainly share in the responsibility to help remedy the situation, but to blame the schools is unfair and unproductive. It is ironic that many parents consider the six or so hours a child spends in school more influential than the other eleven waking hours, much of it taken up with watching TV and playing video games. Some parents seem to be extremely worried about what their kids learn in school while at the same time they are unconcerned about what they learn in front of the TV.

Another popular scapegoat is our legal system. "If judges would get tough with juvenile criminals," some insist, "these problems with our kids wouldn't be happening." Indeed, judges may need to get tougher with youthful offenders as part of the solution to the rising tide of violence among children; but if we think that simply locking up all those who follow violent patterns of behavior is the answer, we're sadly mistaken. We can't build prisons fast enough to solve the problem that way. Even from a perspective of pure self-interest, how can we afford to incarcerate so many of the very people we will need to count on as productive citizens, workers, and taxpayers? If we don't change what we're teaching our kids we'll have the worst of all worlds: rising crime, more and more money spent on prisons, and fewer taxpayers to foot the bill.

Some speak about the deterrent effect of a very strict "get tough" policy against youthful offenders. However, the effectiveness of this strategy, like that of many others, has been greatly weakened because of all the messages that teach children that now is all that matters. Today's kids have been conditioned not to think about consequences.

Our Future At Stake

A significant event occurred in the fall of 1993. On a Friday evening, the Mayor of Washington, D.C. asked the President of the United States to call out the National Guard because the streets of the nation's capitol were "out of control." President Clinton denied the request, and the Guard was not activated. The event was significant nonetheless, because it was another alarm that should tell us how urgent our society's problems have become.

There was no natural catastrophe that night. There was no specific mass civil disturbance, such as the Los Angeles riot. The crisis that prompted the major's request was that the "normal" level of crime and disorder had reached such proportions that the regular police force was judged to be insufficient to contain it.

Although that news report faded from the front page after a few short days, its meaning is profound for our society and for our children. A free democratic society depends on certain characteristics in its citizens for its very survival. Those characteristics include respect for others, the ability to cooperate, self-discipline, and a sense of justice. As those traits begin to disappear, our ability to carry on as a viable society is jeopardized. When we cannot get along as a society, external forces need to be brought in to maintain law and order, and the freedoms of a democracy become more limited. The request by Mayor Kelley should be a warning bell for all of us.

The rapid escalation in concern over violent crime had caused a strong national reaction by 1994. President Clinton and the

Congress passed a "crime control" bill in the summer of that year. The legislation authorized funds for 100,000 additional police officers, and for other law enforcement measures. While those steps may have been necessary, we need to realize they are not the solution. They are another signal that more and more, external force is becoming necessary to control the effects of a problem that is eating away at our nation's soul. Although we may need to apply force as a stop-gap measure, we cannot hope to cure the root of the problem until we address it for what it is: the deterioration of values, particularly among our children.

When it comes to promoting positive values, American society has been avoiding taking action for decades. One reason may be that since we often think of values as being tied into a set of religious beliefs, we as a society have been reluctant to advance a set of values lest a certain religious agenda be forced on everyone. However, the values that are vital to the health of our society transcend all religions and cultures. We can have an articulated, agreed-upon set of values that we can all stand behind as a society no matter how varied our individual backgrounds. Furthermore, we must have one so our social institutions can reinforce the values of our families.

This process of norm setting and norm reinforcement is basic to a well-functioning society. Partly as a result of America's value vacuum, the values of the marketplace have taken over. The powerful voices of American culture have not been reinforcing the values that are necessary for our society to remain strong. Rather, they have been enlisted to promote whatever values increase sales and maximize profits.

What we desperately need to do is identify, teach, and reinforce a set of cultural values that are essential for healthy children and a healthy society. As I've mentioned, these values transcend those of religious denominations. They are the bedrock that we can all subscribe to, regardless of religious affiliation or personal philosophy. As we identify, teach, and reinforce them, these values can be translated into norms that are taught and reinforced by families, communities, and our larger society.

At present, we have individual parents and families teaching a set of values that are undermined by our society. They are contradicted and drowned out by powerful and often technologically advanced voices. When faced with these odds, parents' messages have difficulty competing.

Throughout this book there have been numerous references to conflicting sets of values. On the one hand, we have values that are essential for the survival of a free democratic society. These are often taught and reinforced by parents. On the other hand, we have the values of the marketplace. These are taught by our larger society, through mass media. As we've seen, in too many instances these sets of values are diametrically opposed to one another. Our children are caught in the crossfire, and eventually end up being trained in the values of the marketplace.

I would never presume to prescribe a complete set of values we should all live by. However, there is a list of values with which we can build a broad consensus. The following is a contrast between what our society is teaching our kids and these values:

The Values of the Marketplace	The Values of Healthy Children and a Healthy Society
Anything For Money	*Justice, Fairness*
Win At All Costs	*Respect For Self and Others, Cooperation*
Happiness Equals Wealth	*Self-Esteem From Within*
Instant Gratification	*Self-Discipline*
Self-Interest—Get all You Can	*Altruism, Generosity*

Excess	*Moderation*
Violence As Entertainment	*Peaceful Conflict Resolution, Empathy*
Me First	*Tolerance, Understanding, and Social Responsibility*

While there might be debate about wording or emphasis, I believe that a consensus on healthy values among individuals from all populations already exists. As an example, a July 1993 meeting in Aspen, Colorado of representatives of 30 youth and education organizations agreed on the following "six pillars of character:" respect, trustworthiness, caring, justice, civic virtue, and citizenship.

Given that we can agree as individuals on the values we would like to promote in our children, the discrepancy between that and our society's values are all the more alarming. Until we begin to address the education our children are getting from our popular culture, our expenditures on more police and jails will continue to escalate without providing any real solution.

Just as it would be a mistake to say that we can ignore external remedies and just attend to the underlying value issues, it would likewise be a mistake to ignore our cultural messages and try to solve this crisis by simply handing down tougher sentences and hiring more police. The only truly effective solution will be to use both internal and external means. It is important for us to avoid the "either/or" trap and to confront the problem in both ways. And just as we must use two methods to solve this national problem, so must we commit ourselves to reclaiming America's children both in our own homes and as members of our larger society.

Later in this chapter I will list actions we can take as members of society. Following are some suggestions for parents:

What We Can Do In Our Homes

1. We adults need to be honest with ourselves about the values that we are buying into and teaching our children. As mentioned earlier, we will have little credibility with our children if we teach them to act one way and act another way ourselves. We have to examine our own values and be able to articulate them. Then we need to act consistently according to those values.

2. We need to develop traditions in our families that reinforce core values and provide a counterbalance to the values of the marketplace. Birthdays, holidays, and special occasions, for example, provide an opportunity to help others and give gifts in the form of favors or treats rather than just buying the latest fad items off department store shelves. A coupon given to a child that entitles him or her to breakfast out with a parent, or to an outing with a parent, will be a lot more valuable than the latest toy on the market. Children need to be encouraged to give gifts in the form of favors, too, like a certificate to make and serve breakfast in bed to parents or a sibling. Appreciation of gifts that money can't buy teaches an important lesson.

3. We adults need to examine our priorities in terms of how we spend our time. America's kids need more time with adults who care about them. The term "quality time" has worked its way into our contemporary vocabulary to rationalize the lack of "quantity time," but our kids need both. There is a myth in our culture that tells us we can have it all, but often the ones who suffer the most from that myth are our children. Kids need guidance, nurturing, reassurance, and direction from parents, and they can get it only through a lot of interaction and communication. Kids can't grow up on automatic pilot—they need and deserve the active participation of adults in their lives. Therefore, the time and energy we devote to our children has to be a priority, not whatever is left over when everything else is done.

4. We need to be willing to say "no." It is not the responsibility of kids to set boundaries and limits for themselves—that's the job of adults. There are many voices kids hear that tell them to consume, buy more, do it earlier, and enjoy it all now. Because of kids' natural impatience, they are more than ready to heed those voices. If anyone is going to set the limits so that balance can be maintained, it has to be the adults in a child's life.

As I've said before, I'm not advocating a knee-jerk "no" to everything. Rather, we should have the ability to negotiate with our children when appropriate, but also realize that at some point we have a responsibility to draw the line. It is not an easy thing to do; in the short run, "yes" is a much easier word to say. In the long run, however, "no" can be a much more helpful response.

Some adults are so nervous about coming off as too stern or authoritarian that they hesitate to set limits or say "no." But we can set limits and still keep the lines of communication open. Parents have to maintain standards of behavior, and to do this we must be willing to exercise our authority. Our authoritativeness provides the security and sense of direction that children need. They may grumble and groan about the "nos" they receive, but we need to remember that is their developmental "job." They're supposed to push the limits as they grow to be independent adults. Because they push, that doesn't mean our limits are inappropriate; they must be set and relaxed gradually.

5. We need to be clear about our intolerance for antisocial behavior. We need to ask our teachers and youth leaders to support us when our children are in school or in other activities. Put-downs, foul language, physical attacks on other kids, stealing, vandalism, disregard for others' rights—these are behaviors that need to be confronted immediately because they are expressions of the values of selfishness, greed, and aggression. Children need to be shown consistently that antisocial acts will be dealt with swiftly and that they carry consequences to both the child and those around him.

Our tolerance for these behaviors has grown because they are often modeled in our larger society by celebrities. As a result, the boundary separating appropriate and inappropriate behavior has been blurred. We need to redefine it, and hold our children accountable to maintain it.

6. We cannot afford to turn our children over to electronic babysitters. Television and video games have been misused as child care for too long. We need to know what our kids are watching and playing. As we have seen in earlier chapters, electronic media are very effective value educators. When those media do not promote and teach healthy values, we cannot afford to put our children in their charge. We need to turn off the TV unless there is something to watch that we as parents believe is good for our children to see, and we must monitor our children's use of other media as well. We should know and approve of the movies they are seeing and the music they are listening to.

7. We have to teach our children to be media literate. Since we are living in a technologically sophisticated age, our children need to understand how technology works and how it affects them. For example, children should be taught about how advertising influences them so they are better able to deal with it, and they need to know as soon as possible. We should ask our schools to develop curricula to teach media literacy, and support them in their attempts.

8. We need to teach our children how to think about money. They need to learn that responsibility comes with it. If they always get what they want without budgeting, saving, or waiting, then the marketplace attitude of "Gotta have it now" is reinforced. When children express a strong desire for something that costs money, it is important that on at least some of the occasions they make an investment in it. As has been suggested earlier, they could save up for a percentage of the cost, or adopt the "lay away" approach—the purchasing method whereby an item is set aside with a down payment but isn't actually acquired until it is paid for in full.

We also need to teach our children to share with others. The marketplace message of "What's in it for me?" needs to be balanced with "What can I do to help someone else?" Children should be asked to use a portion of their money to help others, so they can see the value of financial resources in a new light.

9. We need to make sure that our teenagers' jobs do not interfere with more important things. Kids need to understand that their most important tasks are to do their schoolwork and to participate in the upkeep of the household. Extracurricular activities at school can also be important for a teen's social development, and should be encouraged in moderation. Too many kids neglect their schoolwork, household responsibilities, extracurricular opportunities, and even their sleep in order to work for discretionary, nonessential income. We need to make sure our children's priorities are not upside-down. Kids should be told that there is room for an outside job only after other responsibilities are attended to.

10. We parents should link responsibilities with rights; children need to learn that the two go together. Some parents I know have found that it is a wonderful birthday ritual for a child to be given both a new right and a new responsibility each year. For example, the right to cross the street may bring with it the responsibility of bringing the mail in. A child may be allowed to stay up later, but assume the job of taking the garbage out. A girl who is awarded the gift of getting her ears pierced may be expected to put the laundry away. Finally, a driver's license may mean agreeing to share in transporting younger siblings to school or events.

11. We need to read to our children. Enthusiasm for books is best encouraged early in life, before electronic media becomes too distracting. And at the same time we are teaching our children new ideas and skills, we strengthen our bond with them by giving them our time and attention.

12. Particularly with elementary school age children, we need to expose them to heroes who embody healthy values. We need to show them how true heroes help others, and involve them in volunteer programs. This will not only teach them values, but will also add to their variety of experiences, allowing them to "try on lots of different uniforms."

13. We need to stay engaged with our teenagers. While adolescents will naturally be pulling away from us in some ways to assert their growing independence, we need to maintain some connection. We need to engage teens in discussions about values. We need to balance responsibilities with their increasing rights. We should know where their money is coming from and where it's going. And we need to engage teenagers in service to others.

14. Parents need to talk to each other. Parents from around the country all have similar concerns about what's happening to our children. We need to be talking to one another and supporting each other in changing the direction of values education. Parents know better than anyone that they are all our children, and that when fellow parents raise their kids to have positive values, their own children benefit from a healthier peer group.

What We Can—And Must—Do As Members of Society

We have been confronted with societal crises before. When we have been on the brink of disaster, we have rallied together and mobilized our resources to change the direction in which things were going. We have done this when faced with national emergencies. We have even done this in order to deal with public health issues.

The dramatic change in our attitude about tobacco is a clear case in point of how our nation's outlook and behavior can change. A generation ago, tobacco was not only acceptable, it was socially desirable. Magazines ads featured attractive models and celebrities touting this brand of cigarette or that. Many of the characters in movies and TV programs smoked. Then, during the late seventies and the eighties, we as a nation determined that tobacco use was unhealthy and undesirable. Within a decade, an entire nation's attitude changed. A carefully and aggressively pursued health campaign altered society's values about tobacco. Laws were passed regarding how tobacco products could be promoted. Public opinion was shaped by education and constant reinforcement. Today, many smokers feel like they are in a persecuted minority. While we could debate whether they are indeed "persecuted," they are clearly a dwindling minority, because the tide of public opinion has turned one hundred and eighty degrees. Even people who still smoke today by and large report that they wish they didn't.

The anti-tobacco campaign is an example of how successful we can be in shaping attitudes and altering behavior. We could do the same thing with regard to promoting healthy values if we put our minds to it.

In the spring and summer of 1993, the Clinton Administration identified health care reform as the number one domestic issue. Within months, Americans across the country were debating the pros and cons of various reform proposals. Newscasts and public policy shows covered the topic, and it seemed that the nation had become engaged in this important issue. It became the topic of conversation in coffee shops, beauty parlors, and around kitchen tables. And why not? Health care reform affects all of us.

The value crisis confronting our children is every bit as urgent as the need for health care reform. We need to give it a greater priority, and we need to involve everyone in bringing about change. Reclaiming America's children has to become our foremost goal.

On December 17, 1993, a *Los Angeles Times* poll revealed that for the first time, Americans considered crime to be the most serious problem confronting the country. I would suggest that the underlying problem is one of values—of what we are teaching our children. Crime is a great concern, and it needs to be taken seriously. However, we need to remember that crime is a symptom. If we don't also address the underlying issues of injustice and the values vacuum at the same time we fight crime on the streets, then we will be fighting a losing battle.

When it comes to how we as a society sell out America's kids, however, the issue is not just violence and crime. We are teaching our children a warped set of values, and this affects all parts of our lives. We won't stop violence until we stop promoting it. We won't reduce selfishness and greed until we stop glorifying it. We won't eliminate impulsiveness and uncontrolled self-gratification until we reinforce moderation and self-discipline.

In Chapter Two we discussed the dynamics involving moral parents and an immoral society. We explored how individuals with a personal set of values can allow a larger anonymous group with contrary values to carry the day. In our society, the only way that situation can change is for enough of the individuals with conflicting personal values to take a stand. Individual parents, educators, and concerned citizens need to take responsibility for our society by saying: "I want our children to learn these values, and I want my community to support me in this endeavor."

What We Can Do As Members of Society

1. Contribute to Promoting A National Mobilization.

Parents across the country need to commit to a clear set of unambiguous, nondenominational values, and demand that our cultural and government institutions support those values. The effort needs clear support from leaders in every segment of our society, and should include a national summit involving leaders from government, education, churches, social agencies, youth organizations, law enforcement, business, the media, and parent organizations. The process that was used in constructing a health care proposal by the Clinton administration would be a good model. It had broad representation, high visibility, clear objectives, and a timetable. The entire effort was well-publicized and raised the awareness of the entire nation on an important issue.

Such a process would result in a clear plan with specific implementation strategies. That plan should include active involvement by all the institutions involved. For example, PTAs across the country could commit to a program aimed at educating parents on how to counteract negative societal messages. A plan involving schools, government, churches, youth organizations, businesses, and parent groups, focused on reclaiming America's children, would bring about amazing results in terms of greater awareness, motivation to act, and determination to follow through.

We as individuals need to get the ball rolling ourselves. We need to talk to school administrators, school board members, clergy, elected officials and business leaders. The grassroots movement that sprung up around Ross Perot during the presidential campaign of 1992 shows how much influence individuals can have when they begin to raise their voices together. The time has come to do that on behalf of our children.

2. Work to Redirect Media and Advertising

Throughout this book I have talked about the enormous influence that media and advertising have on the values of our children. For the most part, these powerful voices have been used to promote values that sell things and turn a profit. We need to take advantage of the power of media and advertising by enlisting them in a different mission: reclaiming America's children.

The technology of modern media and advertising is powerful. It can be a wonderful ally in teaching our children healthy values. The creativity and knowhow that is currently used to make us unhappy with what we've got could just as easily be employed to help us teach children values like tolerance, cooperation, peaceful conflict resolution, and patience. Program producers and advertisers are rewarded financially for promoting violence, instant gratification, and greed. We need to provide incentives for them to promote the values that will build a strong society by letting our feelings be known.

We need to remember what was discussed in earlier chapters and use it to bring about change. Advertisers and manufacturers are motivated by sales. Currently, they feed our children a diet of violence, instant gratification, and selfishness because it is profitable for them to do so. As soon as it is no longer profitable, they will stop. The economic influence of America's parents can be a potent force for change.

If viewers switch channels, or better yet, turn television sets off and complain to sponsors, we can have an impact. *The Wall Street Journal* reported in 1993 that ABC's violent miniseries *Murder In The Heartland* lost two million dollars after thousands of parents wrote to the sponsors. This shows that advertisers of unhealthy programs will not ignore millions of angry consumers. We need to write to them or call them and let them know that we want a change. And we should not only ask them to stop funding unhealthy programming; we also need to ask them to start funding the creation of programming that will teach important and healthy values to our children.

3. Involve Business Leaders

American business has a financial stake in encouraging healthy values, too. However, this financial stake is long-term; in the short-term, there are profits to be made by promoting marketplace values—those same values that are undermining the character of the workforce of the future. If we are to remain healthy and competitive as a society we need to invest now in healthy human resources for the future: our children.

Business leaders have enormous clout in our country. According to William Greider, author of *Who Will Tell The People?*, they have more than they should have. Nevertheless, that clout can be used to promote change. When parents and educators together with business leaders approach elected officials, advertisers, and media executives, the impact can be substantial. I believe we need to appeal to these business leaders as private citizens. In their business roles, they may be too influenced by their worries about profits. As we have seen, our fixation on profit is what has gotten us into this mess in the first place. However, when we approach them as citizens, as parents, and as grandparents, we will encourage them to relate to concerns about our children and their future.

Business leaders, therefore, need to be included in the effort to reclaim America's children. As we approach them as fellow citizens who have a stake in the well-being of our society, they will be warned that the long-term health of their companies is at risk as well. These leaders have a great deal of influence in our country. They need to join in the enterprise facing us and see it as more than simply good public relations.

4. Support the Establishment of a Cabinet-Level Office Whose Mission is to Safeguard Our Children

In the United States, there are currently fourteen cabinet-level offices charged with creating and administering our nation's policies regarding such things as our natural resources, our energy resources, and our health care policy. If we truly believe that our children are our most precious national resource, we must transform our words into action. I would like to propose the establishment of a cabinet-level post and office to safeguard them.

This office would have powerful symbolic value because it would draw national attention to the importance we place on the treatment of our children. Prior to the energy crisis of the mid 1970s there was no Department of Energy. As our energy needs gained greater prominence, we established a separate department to centralize our efforts to deal with this important area. When the department was established in 1977, it conveyed the importance of energy conservation and energy planning to the entire country.

The Department of Children's Well-Being would have much more than symbolic value, however. The Department would ensure that children's interests are considered when policy decisions are being made. It would be charged with coordinating and funding research on the impact of policies and actions on children. It would be responsible for organizing under one umbrella the offices regarding children that are currently scattered throughout other departments. Joining them into one department would ensure greater coordination and cohesiveness. Another function of the proposed Department of Children's leads to the next recommendation:

5. Advocate Legislation Requiring A Children's Impact Statement On Products and Entertainment

Whenever a construction project is undertaken in our country, the law requires that an environmental impact statement be completed. This is meant to insure that a course of action will not be undertaken until we know what long-term damage might be done to the environment.

Before those laws were enacted, we had many more instances in which expedient or short-sighted actions were taken, which resulted in long-term or permanent damage to the land, air or water. Today, a person who would otherwise find it financially advantageous to release toxins into the water, the air, or the ground has a much greater incentive not to do so. We, as a society, have acknowledged that our country's natural resources deserve some protection.

We also have laws that govern the development and manufacture of drugs. These exist to protect the public as well. A pharmaceutical company cannot bring a new drug to market until it is tested and its effects are known. Even when a drug is approved, the public is informed about possible side effects. These laws are in place to give us reasonable assurance us that the drugs that are prescribed to us are effective and safe when used correctly.

If we have legislation in place to insure that the environment is not harmed, and safeguards to insure us that the drugs doctors prescribe won't harm us, why do we take no similar precautions to insure that the messages sent to our children are not harmful to them?

As a society we need to take our children as seriously as our environment and our pharmaceuticals. We are appropriately outraged to find someone exploiting our resources by dumping toxic material into a river. Yet every day we allow profiteers to exploit our children by dumping toxic material into their minds.

I propose that we protect our children by requiring a "Children's Impact Statement" on products or entertainment that would be "consumed" by children. The Department of Children's Well-Being would be charged with developing standards and the procedures for determining the impact. Producers would be required to complete a Children's Impact Statement according to stated guidelines that would identify objectives, values communicated, benefits, and possible adverse side effects. These statements would then be reviewed by an independent panel for endorsement or for challenge. If the product's impact statement was endorsed, then a statement of endorsement would be distributed with the product. If the panel challenged the manufacturer's statement, a separate, independent impact statement would be completed by the Department of Children's Well-Being. When the product was released, both statements, the manufacturer's and the Department's, would accompany it.

Children's Impact Statements would be available for all products and entertainment directed at children. They would also be compiled and published monthly in a periodical that would be a kind of Consumer Reports for parents.

I would like to stress at this point that I am not recommending censorship. I am calling for information to be provided to the adults who are responsible for watching out for the interests of children.

The proposed system would function much like the Consumers Union, the publisher of *Consumer Reports*. The Consumers Union has existed since 1936, providing consumers with information and advice about goods and services. Products that receive poor evaluations are not banned from the market; they can still be sold. However, the public is better informed and can make more knowledgeable choices based on the Union's independent and unbiased assessment.

Likewise, the proposed Children's Impact Statement and Parents' Consumer Reports would not prevent a product, service, or program from coming to market. That is to say, it would safeguard Constitutional rights and would not result in censorship. It would differ from Consumer Reports in that it would not be administered by a private organization, but rather by the proposed Department of Children's Well-Being.

I believe parents should have access to a Children's Impact Statement on the products and messages aimed at their children. There would be several benefits of such a system. First of all, manufacturers and producers of entertainment would have to be much more conscious of the messages they were delivering to children. They would be made to stop and think about the impact of their products on America's youth. Secondly, parents would be much more aware of the effects of these products on their children, and could make more informed and responsible choices.

There is sure to be some resistance to this suggestion. Some will argue that the inception of Children's Impact Statements and a Department of Children's Well-Being will mean adding to an existing glut of government bureaucracy and increasing government spending. It should be remembered, however, that both liberals and conservatives have already conceded that more government intervention is necessary to address the problems confronting our society. The calls for expanded correctional facilities and more law enforcement certainly involve greater government involvement and more spending. I submit that the dollars directed toward this and some of the other suggestions made in this chapter will undoubtedly be spent more effectively than they would be if we put them into increased law enforcement and more correctional facilities.

6. Work to formulate and pass legislation that protects young children from being exploited as a target market.

Other countries refrain from targeting small children with consumerist pitches. A 1991 article in *Advertising Age* reports that Finland, France, Ireland, Italy, and Portugal have rules restricting the use of children in commercials. In France, for example, children cannot be presenters in a commercial. It is common in these countries to have rules prohibiting the endorsement of a product by children. Spain and Germany do not allow war toys to be advertised. In Sweden, television advertisements cannot be aimed at children under age twelve, and no commercials of any kind can be aired before, during, or after children's programs.

The European community considers advertising to children on a par with advertising for tobacco, alcohol, and pharmaceuticals. It is therefore subject to special regulations. They do this because small children are unable to comprehend how they are being influenced; they have not learned distrust. Targeting preschool children as consumers is unconscionable in many societies, but we do it for profit. We need to stop it.

7. Advocate for and contribute to additional children's programming on noncommercial stations.

It's important to remember that there is some good programming for children, especially on public broadcast stations. We need to have more of it.

Conclusion

The Iroquois Nation has a saying in their treasury of community wisdom. It reads, "In our every deliberation, we must consider the effect of our decision on the next seven generations." We readily acknowledge that this makes sense when we consider the ways in which we treat the earth and the environment—we see how it applies to economic and political decision-making. But nowhere is it more applicable than with regard to the decisions involved in raising our children. The way we as a society treat our children will have lasting implications for generations to come.

Throughout this book I have tried to show how as a society, we exploit our children for financial gain. The driving force behind most of the messages we send to our children is profit. As a result, many unhealthy values are shaped and reinforced. The question of how this affects our children has been largely ignored in the context of our larger society, because in the realm of the market-place, it is an irrelevant question. The only matter of concern in the marketplace is profitability. Consequently, as a society we are not considering the effects of our decisions on "the next seven generations."

When the problems become impossible to miss, it is often tempting to find scapegoats, instead of getting at the real cause. That cause—putting profits over values—is staring us in the face.

The time has come to change that. The time has come to reclaim America's children.

AFTERWORD

As I have presented these ideas in meeting after meeting with parents, the question that comes up repeatedly is "What can we do?" I have tried to provide some suggestions throughout this book, and I would like to offer one additional possibility.

If you are interested in pursuing any of the ideas presented in this book, or if you would simply like to comment on them, please consider filling out the survey enclosed at the end of this book and returning it. Your response will help determine what level of grassroots support various action steps might have. Your completed survey could also be shared with elected officials and other community and business leaders to stimulate further action.

Everyone's involvement is needed to reclaim America's children.

COMMUNITY DISCUSSION QUESTIONS

Dear Reader,

This discussion guide is a tool for you to use to reflect further on the value issues that both you and all of our children face growing up in today's world. This guide can be used individually to help with personal reflection or in a small group setting. Listening and discussing with others in small groups is a great way to come to a better understanding of the problems and their solutions.

Thus we urge you to network with parents and community members on this values crisis in America. The more light we can shine on the roots of this crisis and its effect on our children, the greater likelihood that we as a society will wake up and accept our role in raising healthy children.

Discussion Questions

1. How responsible is the larger community for the health and welfare of its children? What are the responsibilities of the neighborhood; local community/city; state; and larger national society? What types of support should parents expect or demand from these various communities?

2. "Putting a roof over my children's heads and teaching them right from wrong" sums up the opinions of hundreds of parents about their responsibilities toward their children. What are your

family values? Can you list them? What values are important to you in your life outside the family? List.

3. Do you think children will automatically absorb these values from you or do they need to be taught? Discuss.

4. At what age do children begin learning values? Discuss.

5. Think back on your last twenty-four hours. Think of all the ways you've been exposed to the larger society's messages. List them. (Examples may be advertising and other value messages from commercial to the brand name fitted on the outside of your clothes.) What are the values taught and reinforced in these messages?

6. Do these messages support or contradict your earlier list of family and social values? Discuss.

7. How can you as a parent or educator counteract these marketplace values (see chapter 11) and messages? List, then choose two that you will really follow up on.

8. "As a society, we Americans of the late twentieth century are sacrificing our children on the altar of financial gain. We are selling out America's children for money. Although we are often not consciously aware of it, maximizing profit is more important to us than asking ourselves whether or not something is beneficial or harmful to our children." Do you agree or disagree that America is selling out its children? Why or why not?

9. "It would be naive to assert that America's epidemic of violence is simply the result of too much violence in the media; the

roots of violence include racism, poverty, and injustice. It would, however, be equally naive to deny that those roots include society's promotion of violence for profit." Where in your home and neighborhood can you find examples of violence being used to sell a toy, TV show, and so on? List them. How can you limit the violent models your child is exposed to in preschool, elementary age, and the teen years? Discuss.

10. Discuss three concrete ways your community could better support your job as a parent.

List three action steps that you will take in your family to help foster the values that you believe are important for your children.

1. _____

2. _____

3. _____

List three action steps that you will take to help a government body, PTA, or neighborhood group that is working to help foster the values you believe are important for America's Children.

1. _____

2. _____

3. _____

Name _____

Address _____

_____

Congressional District (if known) _____

I, _____ , am deeply concerned about how we, as a society, are "Selling Out America's Children." I support the following: (*Check those you personally support.*)

☐ The Promotion of a National Mobilization Effort on Societal Values
☐ Efforts to Redirect Media and Advertising to Promote Healthy Values For Children
☐ The Involvement of Business Leaders
☐ The Establishment of a Department of Children's Well-Being and a Cabinet-Level Post for the Director of that Department
☐ Children's Impact Statements on Products Marketed to Minors
☐ Legislation Protecting Children From Being Exploited as a Target Market
☐ Funding For Additional Children's Programming On Noncommercial Stations
☐ Other _____

I believe that it is important to promote the following as a set of core, nondenominational values that are essential for healthy children and a healthy society: (*Check all you personally support.*)

☐ Justice, Fairness
☐ Respect for Self and Others
☐ Cooperation
☐ Self-Esteem from Within
☐ Self-Discipline
☐ Altruism, Generosity
☐ Moderation
☐ Peaceful Conflict Resolution
☐ Empathy
☐ Tolerance, Understanding
☐ Social Responsibility
☐ Other _____

☐ Please check here if you would like your name to be on a mailing list for future information.

Please mail to: Reclaiming America's Children
c/o Fairview Press
2450 Riverside Avenue South
Minneapolis, MN 55454

(Please consider sharing your completed survey with elected officials and other community and business leaders)

INDEX

teachers
modeling values, 46
problems facing, 138
teenagers
careers, ideas about
successful, 114-15,
120-21
staying engaged with, 148
time spent with
fathers, 25
violence and, 1-2, 6, 62
working, 121-22, 147
television
aggressive behavior
and, 75
alternatives to, 59
appropriate use of, 57-60
children targeted by
advertisers, 39-41
consumerism promoted
through, 37-38, 116-17
as de facto babysitter,
27, 146
effects on children's
development, 55-56,
76
major themes of, 51
as marketing tool, 50-51
monitoring usage, 146
noncommercial stations
for children, 158
"parent chip," 78
in schools, 49
values transmitted by,
47-49, 52, 74-76
viewing habits,
children's, 47-48

violence, 51, 52, 56-57,
67-69
"throwaway society,"
90-91
tobacco, 5, 119
anti-tobacco campaign,
149
tolerance, 97, 143
toys, violence and, 72-73
traditions, developing
healthy, 144

unwed mothers, 28-29

values
cultural value
messages (*see* cultural
value messages)
deterioration of, 141-43
excess as societal value,
103
generosity to
self-absorption, shift
from, 127
group behavior and
individual, 12-13
marketplace, 142-43
materialism as
societal value, 113-16
parental values
compared to
societal, 14, 137
parents as teachers of,
22, 45-46
positive values (*see*
positive values)
"six pillars of
character," 143